HELL'S KITCHEN COOKBOOK

GRANADA

Ventures

Acknowledgements

Hell's Kitchen is a major television production, recorded live and utilising the expertise of 300 cast and crew, without whose dedicated efforts nothing would be possible. The Publisher would like to thank the following at Granada for their invaluable help in the production of this book: Layla Sabih, Jason Tann, John Hollywood, Jeanette Moffat and Hayley Chapman and Kevin Morgan and Shana White at Granada Ventures.

Thanks to Mike Kenny at Component Graphics, creators of the Hell's Kitchen programme graphics, and Kieron McCarron for his behind-the-scenes photography.

Thanks to Beverly LeBlanc and Roz Denny for additional recipe contributions and to Maria Malone for writing the show resume. Finally, thanks to Dan Jones for photography, Roisin Nield for styling, Eliza Baird and her assistant Debbie Dalgliesh for food styling and all at Smith & Gilmour for design.

The nutritional information in this book is for reference only. The recipes and any suggestions are to be used at the reader's sole discretion and risk. Always consult a doctor if you are in any doubt about nutritional or medical conditions. Chefs' and contestants' recipes were originally designed for restaurant production. Where appropriate the publisher has amended quantities for use in domestic preparation.

First published in Great Britain in 2005 by
Virgin Books Ltd
Thames Wharf Studios
Rainville Road
London
W6 9HA

Hells Kitchen
A Granada Production Ltd © 2005
Licensed by Granada Ventures Ltd

A catalogue record for this book is available from the British Library.

ISBN 0 7535 1098 7

The paper used in this book is a natural, recyclable product made from wood grown in sustainable forests. The manufacturing process conforms to the regulations of the country of origin.

Designed and typeset by Smith & Gilmour, London

Printed and bound in Great Britain by Bath Press

CONTENTS

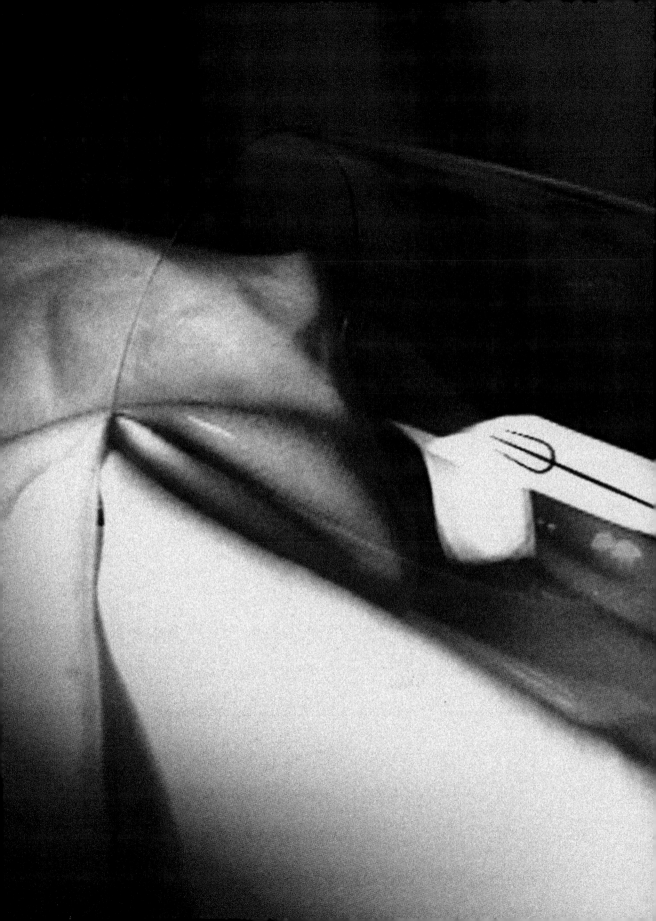

WELCOME TO
HELL'S KITCHEN

It must rank as one of the most bizarre restaurants in London. Run by first-rate chefs with a clutch of Michelin stars between them, the menu is mouthwatering, but there's no guarantee diners will actually get anything to eat. The food that does make it from the kitchen to the tables can range from the sublime to the inedible. Those fortunate enough to eat may have to wait hours before whatever they've ordered arrives and, even then, what they get may not be what they asked for in the first place. A simple three-course meal can soon degenerate into chaos. The arrival of a starter, for instance, doesn't necessarily mean a main course will follow. It can all be extremely hit and miss. Yet hungry, hopeful celebrities turn up night after night simply because this has become the place to eat (or not). For two weeks only, diners willingly risk culinary mayhem for a table at the hottest restaurant in town, safe in the knowledge that, whatever happens, there is one consolation – it's all free.

When the restaurant opened for business in a converted warehouse in London's East End in 2004, launching a new reality show on ITV, it became, quite literally, an overnight success. Running the kitchen was Gordon Ramsay, a chef with three coveted Michelin stars to his name. As well as a reputation for innovative cooking, Ramsay was renowned for his no-nonsense attitude and colourful language. He had agreed to take ten celebrities – not averse to being shouted and sworn at – and attempt to turn them into chefs, all in the space of a fortnight. It was possibly the greatest challenge of his professional life and, predictably, it didn't go entirely to plan.

When Hell's Kitchen opened the celebrity diners came, lured by the prospect of a (free) meal cooked by a man regarded by many as London's finest restaurateur. In the first few days of business, however, the restaurant was less than the culinary success Ramsay had hoped for. As the celebrity chefs slaved away in the kitchen, many of the diners went hungry.

Not everyone was convinced that even Gordon Ramsay, despite his fearsome reputation, would make chefs of his trainees. On the face of it they were an unlikely bunch, not cut out for a regime of long, arduous days toiling in a busy kitchen. Ramsay was utterly serious about turning Hell's Kitchen into a fine restaurant. Only one thing mattered – serving first-rate food. The fact this might prove beyond the capabilities of a bunch of unskilled and inexperienced trainees was of no concern. They had to learn. fast. Ramsay bawled at them and hurled insults. His fury knew no bounds, and the presence of TV cameras did nothing to temper his outbursts. Only the strongest and most able would survive.

Broadcaster Roger Cook suffered an early injury and was the first to bow out. Sprinter Dwain Chambers took off just as things were warming up, as did Tommy Vance. Former politician Edwina Currie hung on until the public voted her out, but managed to drive Ramsay mad in the process. Actress Amanda Barrie almost came to blows with him. Singer Belinda Carlisle was reduced to tears. Ramsay's methods were vindicated, however when his would-be chefs – including comedian Al Murray, singer Matt Goss, and glamour girl Abi Titmuss – started getting it right. Actor James Dreyfus – to everyone's surprise – knuckled down too. The undisputed star, though, was Jennifer Ellison, whose signature dish of steak and chunky chips won over the diners and the TV viewers. The youngest trainee, she emerged the winner.

One year on, in spring 2005, Hell's Kitchen prepared to open its doors again.

This time ten members of the public with a passion for food would be pitted against one another in two teams. There would be two head chefs, not one. The restaurant, which had started life as a baroque dining room, had undergone a complete transformation. Second time around, designer Markus Blee struck a more contemporary note, using mirrors and curved walls. In charge of the red kitchen, Gary Rhodes, who rose to the top of his profession at the tender age of 26 with his first Michelin star (since then, four more have come his way, most recently for his London restaurant, Rhodes 24). In a career spanning almost thirty years, Rhodes has risen to dizzy heights, priding himself in simple British fare like Welsh rarebit and bread-and-butter pudding. Where food is concerned, he is a self-confessed perfectionist. Nothing less will do, as his team of trainees soon discovered.

Gary Rhodes went into Hell's Kitchen determined to maintain the sort of standard diners have come to expect of him. 'It's a question of treating it as a professional kitchen,' he said. 'This is a brand-new restaurant. We've got an opening time. We've got to be ready. We've got to have the menu complete.'

Among the gastronomic glitterati,
Gary Rhodes is widely acknowledged as the jewel in the crown of British cooking. According to Michel Roux, *chef de cuisine* of Le Gavroche, 'he's probably the best chef that Britain has ever had'.

It is a view echoed by Raymond Blanc, *chef patron* of Le Manoir Aux Quat' Saisons. 'I think Gary, technically, is one of the very best chefs in the country, there's no doubt about that.'

Taking him on, Jean-Christophe Novelli – as French as Rhodes is British – whose swarthy, film-star looks once led to him being voted sexiest man in the world. Novelli would run the blue kitchen with panache, savoir-faire and a dash of *je ne sais quoi*. In terms of style and substance, the two men could not be more different: one an exponent of all things British, one the epitome of all things French. One disciplined, the other flamboyant. Rhodes striving for perfection in the kitchen, Novelli driven by passion. Where Gary Rhodes would choose the simple approach, Jean-Christophe would prefer to make his food as complex as possible. Michel Roux describes Jean-Christophe as the pop star of French cooking. 'He's got the curls, the looks. He is a French cockerel,' says Roux.

Restaurateur Marco Pierre White, a fan of the Frenchman, says he is driven by emotion. 'He's a person who cooks from his heart, not his mind . . . I think Gary will be more clinical, he'll play a safer game. Jean will play a higher-risk strategy. He'll make life very hard. He can't help himself.'

As for the opposition, Rhodes said, 'Jean-Christophe? He's got great respect in the industry, more for his looks, I think, than for his cooking.'

Jean-Christophe, a frown clouding his handsome features, said, 'Gary Smith? Non. Gary White? Ah, Gary *Rhodes*!'

Having weighed each other up in less than flattering terms, the challenge for each chef was to turn their team of five trainees into first-rate cooks in the space of just two weeks. Each night blue and red kitchens would compete to serve the best food to the most diners, and each night the diners would give their verdict. As the series progressed, viewers would vote off the trainees until just two remained, each competing for a grand prize of £250,000 with which to open their own restaurant.

With so little time and so much at stake, competition was intense from the outset. For Gary Rhodes and Jean-Christophe Novelli, their pride and reputations on the line, the battle for Hell's Kitchen would be closely fought at every stage. Both chefs were to prove uncompromising and, at times, brutal taskmasters. Plates would be thrown, as well as accusations and abuse. As the pressure mounted and the lack of sleep took its toll, the trainees would eventually turn on one another. Those who stuck it out, however, became extraordinarily good, extraordinarily fast. And all emerged with respect for their mentors.

Each day would bring drama, disappointment, frustration and – for those who made it to the end – ultimately, euphoria. It was, for all concerned, the culinary challenge of their lives.

When Gary Rhodes and Jean-Christophe Novelli unveiled their menus for Hell's Kitchen they could not have been more different. The most popular dishes from the series have been adapted to work at home, without the one staple ingredient all the trainees had to contend with – a shouting, swearing head chef breathing down their necks!

STARTERS

GARY RHODES

Smoked Haddock Topped with Welsh Rarebit on a Plum Tomato and Chive Salad

SERVES 4

300 g plum tomatoes, blanched and peeled
Some finely chopped chives
Basic vinaigrette (see Basics, page 99)
4 fillets smoked haddock, about 125g each

FOR WELSH RAREBIT MIX:
250 g mature Cheddar, grated
50 ml milk
15 g plain flour

2 tablespoons fresh white breadcrumbs
1 teaspoon English mustard powder
A shake of Worcestershire sauce
2 eggs
2 egg yolks
Sea salt and freshly ground white pepper

First, make the rarebit. Put the cheese into a nonstick saucepan with the milk. Heat slowly until the cheese melts, stirring to mix in the milk. As the mixture begins to bubble, stir in the flour, breadcrumbs, mustard and Worcestershire sauce.

Cook for a minute or so, taking care not to let it boil. The mixture should form a ball. Remove and cool until cold.

Tip into a food processor and process, slowly adding the eggs and yolks. Scoop out into a bowl and chill, then tip this mixture out between two large sheets of nonstick baking parchment and roll into a 3 mm thickness. Cut out four portions, enough to fit over the haddock portions. Use a sharp knife dipped in water for even sides. You may have leftover rarebit which can be used elsewhere (even on toast!).

Slice tomatoes thinly and arrange on four plates in the centre as overlapping rounds. Season nicely.

Preheat a grill. Lay the haddock portions in a large buttered heatproof dish and top each with the rarebit. Grill for about 5 minutes until just firm, golden and bubbling.

Sprinkle the tomatoes with vinaigrette and the chives and sit a bubbling haddock fillet on top.

Seared Scallops with Creamy Mashed Potatoes and 'Devilled Sauce'

SERVES 4

1 quantity creamed mashed potato
(see Basics, see page 97)
12 large scallops
Olive oil
A little lemon juice

FOR THE SAUCE:
250 g shallots, finely chopped
25 g butter

1 teaspoon demerara sugar
Small pinches of cayenne pepper
A good pinch of crushed black pepper
200 ml red Cabernet Sauvignon vinegar
300 ml white wine
300 ml veal stock (see Basics, page 94)
2 level teaspoons English mustard
Salt and pepper

1 First, make the sauce. Sweat the shallots in the butter with the sugar until they take on a rich golden-caramel brown. Add the cayenne and crushed black pepper and cook for 2 minutes.

2 Pour in the vinegar and cook until reduced right down until almost dry. Pour in the wine, and boil until reduced by three-quarters.

3 Add the veal stock and bring to a gentle simmer. Cook for about 15 minutes and mix in half the mustard and seasoning to taste. Taste the sauce for strength and add more mustard if you can take the heat! Set aside.

4 Make the mashed potato. When ready to serve, heat a little oil in a heavy-based frying or griddle pan. Season the scallops then fry for about 2 minutes each side until just cooked and still a little bouncy. Don't overcook. Squeeze over a little lemon juice.

5 Pipe the potato at the top end of four warmed shallow serving bowls. Spoon sauce in the centre of the bowls, then sit scallops on top.

'Everything has fallen into place wonderfully. As for Aaron on the starters, he was giving me scallops to die for … just unbelievable.' Gary Rhodes

English Breakfast Salad with a Warm Poached Egg and Crisp Salad Leaves

SERVES 4

8 new potatoes, boiled and halved

50 g unsalted butter

200 g bacon lardons

4 slices black pudding, 1 cm thick

4 fresh large free-range eggs

A little white wine vinegar

4 rounds of crisp toast, buttered

100 g bag mixed salad leaves

FOR THE DRESSING:

100 ml olive oil

2 teaspoons Dijon mustard

2 tablespoons red wine vinegar

1 tablespoon chopped chives

Sea salt flakes and freshly ground white pepper

1 First, make the dressing by whisking together the oil, mustard, vinegar and seasoning, then mix in some chives. Set aside.

2 Fry the potato halves in the butter until golden and crisp on both sides and set aside.

3 Fry the bacon lardons in the same pan until crispy and the fat starts to run. Mix with the potatoes and keep warm.

4 Fry the black pudding in the same pan for about 2 minutes each side until crisp, then remove, cut each piece in 2 or 4 and keep warm.

5 Pick over the salad leaves and toss with half the dressing.

6 Bring a pan of water to the boil and add the white wine vinegar and some salt. Crack the eggs into a cup each. As the water starts to boil, swirl it into a vortex with a wooden spoon and immediately slide the eggs in one at a time. They will set in neat teardrop shapes as the water spins. Turn the heat down to a bare simmer and cook the eggs for 2 to 3 minutes until just set.

7 Immediately remove with a slotted spoon and pat dry with some paper towel. If you have time, you can trim them to a neat shape with kitchen scissors.

8 To serve, put the buttered toasts in the centre of four warmed plates and top with the eggs. Season. Arrange the potatoes, lardons and black pudding around the eggs and put neat piles of salad on top of the egg. Drizzle over the last of the dressing and serve.

Pan-Fried Sea Bass with Blackberry Shallots and Creamy Hollandaise Sauce

SERVES 4
4 sea bass fillets, about 150 g each, skin on
A little flour, for dusting
1 tablespoon vegetable oil
A knob of butter
FOR THE BLACKBERRY SHALLOTS:
2 large (banana) shallots
300 ml red wine
3 tablespoons crème de mure
Olive oil, for serving
FOR THE SAUCE:
500 ml hollandaise sauce (see Basics, page 100)
100 ml double cream, lightly whipped
Sea salt and pepper

1 First, make the blackberry shallots. Slice the shallots into 3 mm rings. Mix with the wine and crème de mure for about 12 hours. Then transfer everything to a heavy-based saucepan and cook slowly until softened.

2 Drain the shallots and reserve the liquid. Season the shallots while you return the liquid to the pan and boil down until syrupy. Set aside.

3 Make the hollandaise. Keep warm in a bain-marie, i.e. a bowl set over warm water. When ready to serve, toss the fish in seasoned flour to coat, shaking off excess. Heat the oil in a large frying pan and cook skin-side first for 4 to 5 minutes on a medium heat without shaking the pan for a nice crisp finish.

4 Slide in a knob of butter and carefully turn the fish to cook the other side. Whip the cream until just floppy and fold into the hollandaise.

5 Reheat the shallots (in a microwave is fine) and spoon into the centre of four warmed plates. Sit a fish fillet on top of each plate and drizzle around the reduced sauce and some olive oil. Serve the sauce alongside.

White Cherry Tomato Soup with Mozzarella and Tapenade Toasts

SERVES 4

600 g cherry tomatoes, quartered
1 x 400 g can chopped plum tomatoes
100 ml double cream
A good pinch of sea salt and freshly
ground white pepper

FOR THE TAPENADE:
60 g black olives, stoned
1 small garlic clove, crushed
3 tinned anchovy fillets, patted dry
2 teaspoons capers, drained
2 teaspoons olive oil
A squeeze of fresh lemon juice

FOR THE TOMATO DRESSING
2 plum tomatoes, halved
1 slice of garlic
A little extra olive oil

TO SERVE:
Round slices of mozzarella
Round slices of toast
Cherry tomatoes and some chopped
tomato
Fresh basil leaves and rocket
Parmesan shavings

1 First make the soup. Roughly chop the fresh tomatoes and blitz in a food processor with the canned tomatoes and salt to taste until smooth and creamy. Lay a large clean muslin cloth in a big sieve or colander over a deep bowl. Pour the tomato purée into the sieve and allow to drip through overnight.

2 Next morning, gently draw up and squeeze the muslin to extract any more juice. You should have a lovely translucent tomato liquid. Discard the solids.

3 When ready to serve, gently heat the tomato liquid and mix in the cream. Use a stick blender to gently pulse the liquid, blending to a smooth creamy texture. Check the seasoning and set aside.

4 Next, make the tapenade. Crush the olives, garlic, anchovies and capers in a pestle and mortar, mixing in the olive oil and lemon juice at the end and seasoning with pepper only. Or, blitz in a small food processor. Set aside.

5 For the tomato dressing, pan-fry the tomatoes in some olive oil until well coloured and softened. Then rub them through a sieve with the back of a ladle, adding a little olive oil to loosen. You can spoon this into a small plastic squeezy bottle to squirt out in neat lines, or drizzle it from a teaspoon.

6 When you are ready to serve, spread some tapenade on the toasts, top with mozzarella and grill lightly until melted. Scatter with some chopped tomato. Place on a serving plate. Halve the cherry tomatoes and sit alongside the toasts drizzled with some tomato dressing, basil and rocket leaves. Finally reheat the soup and pour into demitasse cups to sit on the same plates.

BLUE MENU
JEAN-CHRISTOPHE NOVELLI

Smoked Pork Knuckle with Foie Gras, Shitake Mushrooms and Savoy Cabbage

SERVES 8 TO 10

FOR THE STOCK:
6 smoked pork knuckles
1 kg finely chopped vegetables
(onions, carrots and celery)
3 sprigs fresh thyme
Half a head of garlic
8 litres water
Handful of fresh parsley stalks
Seasoning

FOR THE FILLING:
Melted duck fat or olive oil, for frying

300 g chopped onions
2 garlic cloves
15g fresh thyme sprigs
100 g duck gizzards or chicken livers, chopped roughly
75 g shitake mushrooms, sliced
10 outer leaves Savoy cabbage
30 g flat parsley and chervil, chopped
1 sprig fresh sage, chopped
1 sprig fresh tarragon, chopped
200 g foie gras

1 Soak the knuckles for 12 hours in cold water, changing the water 3 or 4 times. Then drain, place in a large stockpot with the vegetables, thyme, garlic, parsley stalks and pepper. Cover with the water. Bring slowly to the boil then simmer for about 2 ½ hours until the meat is very tender.

2 Cool in the stock, then lift out the knuckles and carefully remove the skin, keeping it as whole as possible (you need it for rolling later). Shred the meat and reserve. Strain the stock and boil to reduce down by half, then measure off 250 ml for the filling. Use the rest elsewhere.

3 To make the filling, heat some duck fat or oil in a large pan and gently sweat the onions with the garlic and thyme sprigs until softened. Add the gizzards or the livers and fry for a couple of minutes more until just firm. Add the 250 ml stock and cook until reduced right down. Remove and cool.

4 Heat more oil in another pan and fry off the sliced shitakes.

5 Cut out the thick base core of the cabbage-leaf stalks. Blanch the cabbage leaves in boiling salted water until just softened, then drain, pat dry and fry in more duck fat or oil for a couple of minutes.

6 Heat a nonstick frying pan until hot and pan-fry the foie gras for a couple of minutes each side until lightly browned (it doesn't need extra fat or oil for frying). Don't overcook, then slice thinly.

7 Stir together the onion–liver mix, shitakes, shredded pork knuckle meat and foie gras. Check the seasoning; you may not need much salt.

8 Now, scrape the inside of the knuckle skin to remove all the fat. Lay out on a large sheet of clingfilm and place the cabbage leaves on top.

9 Put the knuckle mixture on top, spreading to the edges, then roll up tightly in the clingfilm and chill until firm. Cut in slices to serve.

Steamed Wild Mushroom and Poppy-seed Pancake Gateaux with Cep Emulsion and Parmesan Crackling

SERVES 6

75 g shitake mushrooms

75 g oyster mushrooms

75 g button mushrooms

50 g Portobello mushrooms

25 g chestnut mushrooms

Olive oil, for frying

1 teaspoon butter

1 shallot, chopped

1 garlic clove, chopped

5 g each flat-leaf parsley and chives, chopped

5 g each fresh tarragon or thyme leaves, chopped

FOR THE CHICKEN MOUSSE:

120 g chicken breast

150 ml double cream

1 egg

75 g cured foie gras, diced

FOR THE PANCAKES:

2 eggs

40g flour

3 tablespoons milk

2 teaspoons poppy seeds

FOR THE EGG CUSTARD:

1 large egg

160ml single cream

TO SERVE:

Delicious served with either cep velouté or port sauce and parmesan crackling (see Basics, page 96, 97 , 103)

1 Wash and slice all the mushrooms then pat dry. Pan-fry in hot olive oil with the butter until lightly browned, seasoning well.

2 Mix together the shallots, garlic and herbs, then set aside to marinate.

3 To make the chicken mousse, chill a food processor or blender bowl and trim excess sinew from the chicken. Blitz the chicken flesh in the processor or blender, adding a little sea salt to taste. Remove the bowl to the fridge and chill for 10 minutes, then blitz again, scraping down the sides. Repeat three times more. Then blitz again, gradually mixing in the egg then the cream, in a slow stream. Rub the mixture through a sieve so it is extra-smooth and season again.

4 Make the pancakes. Beat together the eggs and flour, gradually beating in the milk then the poppy seeds. Make 6 thin pancakes, in the usual way. Cover and keep warm.

5 For the egg custard, simply mix everything together well and let stand for 10 minutes.

6 Now you can assemble the gateaux. Line 6 dariole moulds or ramekins, 120 ml capacity, with clingfilm and press in a pancake so it overhangs the edge. Spoon in a little mushroom mix, then drizzle over some custard and spoon in chicken mousse (adding a little diced foie gras, if liked).

7 Fold in the pancake, cover tightly in clingfilm and steam for 15 minutes. Demould to serve, surrounded by a mixture of pan-fired wild mushrooms according to availability and a sauce, either ceps or port sauce. Garnish with parmesan crackling, if liked.

Seared Baby Squid, Tiger Prawn and Lemon Grass Brochette with Beetroot and Roquette Salad

SERVES 4

8 baby squid
8 raw large tiger prawns
3 sticks lemon grass
16 lemon balm or mint leaves
75 g shitake mushrooms
2 large beetroots
300 ml red wine
2 teaspoons sugar
8 cherry tomatoes (optional)
Olive oil, for sprinkling
Leaves from 2 sprigs of fresh thyme
100 g rocket leaves
100 g mizuna leaves
10 basil leaves, torn in pieces
A little vinaigrette dressing (see Basics, page 99)
Seasoning

1 Wash the baby squid under a cold running tap, pull off the head and tentacles then pull out the translucent backbone inside the body cavity. Wash inside the cavity and trim the opening.

2 Pull off the heads from the prawns and peel. Slice the mushrooms. Peel the outer layer of lemon grass, trim the tops and split in half to make thin skewers.

3 Make 4 brochettes of squid, prawns, mushrooms and lemon balm leaves. Set aside.

4 Wash the beetroot and boil, unpeeled, in salted water for 20 minutes, then peel. Grate on a coarse grater, then cook the grated flesh in the red wine with the sugar and seasoning until the wine is reduced by half.

5 Halve the cherry tomatoes, season and sprinkle with some oil and the thyme leaves. Set in a low oven for 30 minutes to dry out a little.

6 When ready to serve, heat a little oil in a griddle pan and cook the brochettes for about 5 minutes, turning once.

7 Dress the rocket, mizuna and basil leaves with a little dressing and arrange on four plates with the tomatoes on top (optional). Sit the brochettes on top and the beetroot salad alongside.

Pan-fried Boudin Noir and Seared Scallops with Crushed Ratte Potatoes, Apple Crisps and Horseradish Velouté

SERVES 4

4 Ratte potatoes (use Charlotte potatoes if not available)

1 shallot, chopped fine

1 teaspoon white wine vinegar

½ Granny Smith apple, cored and diced finely

4 apples crisps (see Basics, page 175)

10 g fresh grated horseradish

3 tablespoons double cream

Juice of 1 lemon

4 slices of black pudding

4 medium scallops, cleaned

Olive oil, for frying

50 g rocket

1 tomato, seeded and finely chopped

½ teaspoon truffle oil

Sprigs of chervil and tips of chives, to serve

Seasoning

1 Cook the potatoes until just tender, then peel and return to the pan. Crush with a fork then mix with the shallot, vinegar and diced apple. Season and set aside.

2 Mix together the horseradish, cream, lemon juice and seasoning.

3 Pan-fry the black pudding and scallops in olive oil, taking care not to overcook. Season in the pan.

4 Mix together the rocket, chopped tomato, seasoning and truffle oil.

5 To serve, divide the crushed potatoes on 4 plates. Top with the scallops then the dried apple slices, black pudding, rocket and tomato and finish with the chervil and chives.

Roulade of Goats' Cheese, Sweet Red Peppers and Aubergine

SERVES 4 TO 6

1.5 kg baking potatoes, e.g. Maris Piper
Olive oil, for frying
About 500 g duck or goose fat
1 celeriac, about 500g
2 garlic cloves, crushed
3 medium aubergines
A little sugar
4 red peppers
A few tips of thyme and oregano
500 g mature goats' cheese in a log, sliced thinly

500 g firm mozzarella sliced thinly
2 teaspoons truffle oil
2 teaspoons garlic oil (see Basics, page 111)
125g fresh basil leaves
50g fresh tarragon leaves
50g fresh mint leaves
1 portion tapenade (see Basics, page 101)
Seasoning

1 Peel the potatoes then slice thinly using a Japanese mandoline. Pan-fry half the potatoes in some olive oil until golden brown, then drain. Confit (i.e. cook gently) the remaining potatoes in a deep pan with the duck fat until softened.

2 Drain, reserving the fat and pouring it back into the pan.

3 Peel and thinly slice the celeriac in the same way, then confit these slices also in the reserved duck fat with the garlic.

4 Slice the aubergines lengthways thinly into 8 and cook gently in olive oil, seasoning with salt, pepper and the sugar until softened. Drain and set aside.

5 Quarter the peppers, core and lay on a baking tray. Drizzle with more oil and sprinkle with the thyme leaves and oregano with seasoning. Cover loosely with foil and cook in an oven at about 180°C/Gas 4 for about 20 minutes until softened. Then cool and peel.

6 Pick over the basil leaves and destalk. Slice the two cheeses.

7 To assemble as roulades, cover a worktop or table with two large sheets of clingfilm. Arrange the golden fried potatoes down the centre in a wide overlapping line. Then make layers of confit potatoes and celeriac, the two cheeses (sprinkled with seasoning, truffle and garlic oils), aubergines, red peppers, basil, tarragon and mint leaves and tapenade. Repeat the layers until you have a depth of about 12 cm.

8 Now, tightly roll over the clingfilm – this will require two people – and twist both ends into a firm roll, making sure there are no air gaps. Tie both ends with string. Stab one end a couple of times with a knife tip and hang up allowing the juices to drip out. This ensures the roulade will be firm to slice.

Spiced Crab Salad with Mango and mini-poppadums

SERVES 4 TO 6

- 60 g cucumber
- 1 stalk lemon grass
- 60 g creamed coconut
- 4 tablespoons boiling water
- finely grated rind and juice of 1 lime
- 1 red chilli
- 1 large fresh mango, ideally Alfonso
- Several sprigs fresh coriander leaves

- Several sprigs fresh mint leaves
- 300 g fresh white crabmeat, picked over
- Salt and pepper
- Lime wedges
- TO SERVE:
- Sunflower oil
- 18 to 24 mini-poppadums
- Crisp Romaine lettuce leaves

Cut the cucumber in half and scoop out the seed in the centre with a small teaspoon. Cut the halves into long strips about 5 mm thick, then into equal-sized dice. Put in a colander in the sink, sprinkle with salt and set aside for 20 to 30 minutes.

Meanwhile, remove the tough outer layers of the lemon grass, then pound with the handle of a knife to bruise; set aside. Deseed and finely chop the chilli; set aside.

Crumble the creamed coconut into a heatproof bowl large enough to hold all the salad ingredients and stir in the water until the coconut dissolves. Add the lemon grass, chilli and lime rind and lime juice to taste. Set aside to cool completely, then cover and chill until required.

Peel the mango, cut off the sides and remove the stone. Roughly dice the flesh the same size as the cucumber and set aside. Rinse the cucumber and pat dry. Remove the coriander and mint leaves from the stalks and tear into small pieces.

Remove the lemon grass from the dressing and discard. Flake the crabmeat into the dressing. Add the cucumber, mango, chilli and herbs and toss together. Add salt and pepper to taste. Cover and chill until ready to serve.

Heat at least 7.5cm depth of sunflower oil to 180°C. Add the mini-poppadums and fry for about 1 minute, or according to the pack instructions, until they are golden brown and crisp. Use a slotted spoon to remove from the oil and drain well on crumpled kitchen paper; leave to cool.

Shred the Romaine lettuce leaves into julienned strips, then divide between glass bowls or cocktail glasses. Spoon the crab salad on top and add a lime wedge. Serve with the mini-poppadums on the side.

Asparagus Velouté
with Chive-onion oil

SERVES 4 TO 6

800 g asparagus

1 large shallot

30 g unsalted butter

600 ml vegetable stock, boiling

150 ml thick crème fraiche

1 medium egg yolk

Salt and white pepper

Chive-onion oil, see below

Fresh snipped chives, to garnish

1 Snap off the woody end of each asparagus spear, then use a vegetable peeler to remove any tough outer layers. Chop the asparagus tips and stalks and set aside. Peel and finely chop the shallot.

2 Melt the butter in a saucepan over medium heat. Add the shallot and stir around for 3 minutes, or until soft. Stir in the chopped asparagus.

3 Add the stock with a little salt and white pepper. Bring to the boil, then reduce the heat and simmer for 20 minutes, or until the pieces of stalk are very tender.

4 Transfer the contents of the pan to a large mouli-legume and purée into another pan, or purée the soup in a food processor and work it through a fine sieve. Return the pan to the heat and bring to the boil, stirring, then reduce the heat and simmer.

5 Stir this mixture into the soup, whisking constantly, but do not allow to boil. Taste and adjust seasoning.

6 Ladle the soup into 4 to 6 hot soup bowls, then drizzle with chive-onion oil. Sprinkle with chives and serve at once.

CHIVE-ONION OIL

MAKES ABOUT 80 ML

40 g fresh chives

1 spring onion, coarsely chopped

120 ml olive oil

1 Blanch the chives and spring onion in a saucepan of boiling water for 30 seconds. Drain and transfer to a bowl of ice water. Remove and pat dry.

2 Heat the oil over medium heat until it is warm and the surface just shimmers. Put the chives and spring onion in a blender or food processor and blitz until well chopped, then add the oil and blitz again. Transfer to a bowl, cover with clingfilm and leave to infuse at room temperature for at least 4 hours.

3 Strain the oil into a bowl, without pressing with a spoon, then transfer to a squeezy bottle with a fine tip. Store at room temperature for up to a week.

Mixed Julienned Vegetables and Seafood in Saffron Broth with Melba Toast

SERVES 4 TO 6

Small pinch of saffron threads

100 g boneless monkfish

100 g salmon fillet

4 red mullet fillets, about 60 g each

4 large queen scallops, with coral if liked

1 carrot

1 celery stick

1 courgette, rinsed

100 ml dry white wine, such as Chablis

100 ml fish stock

40 g unsalted butter

1 small shallot

1 garlic clove

1 sprig fresh dill, 1 sprig fresh chervil,

1 spring fresh flat-leaf parsley and 1 bay leaf, tied together into a bouquet garni

150 ml crème fraîche

Salt and white pepper

Chopped fresh chervil to garnish

Melba toast, see below

1 Lightly toast the saffron threads in a dry frying pan over medium-high heat just until you smell the aroma. Immediately tip the saffron out of the pan and set aside.

2 Remove any skin and the thin membrane covering the monkfish, then slice into medallions about 1 cm thick. Remove any skin from the salmon fillet and cut into thin slices. Using a thin, sharp knife, slice the scallops horizontally into 2 or 3 slices depending on the thickness. Cover the seafood and chill until required.

3 Peel the carrot, then cut the carrot, celery and courgette into thin julienne slices; set aside.

4 Put the wine and fish stock in a saucepan and boil for about 2 minutes; set aside.

5 Melt the butter in a sauté pan over a medium heat. Add the shallot and garlic, bouquet garni and prepared vegetables with salt and white pepper to taste. Sauté for 3 minutes.

6 Pour over the reduced stock and wine, reduce the heat and simmer for 3 to 5 minutes until the vegetables are soft.

7 Add the seafood to the pan, cover and simmer over medium-low heat for 3 to 5 minutes until all the seafood is cooked through and flakes easily. Take care not to overcook.

8 Use a slotted spoon to transfer the fish to a warm bowl, spoon over a little of the cooking liquid, then cover tightly with foil and set aside.

Stir the crème fraîche and saffron threads into the cooking broth and bring to the boil, stirring. Boil for 3 minutes or until the liquid reduces. Taste and adjust the seasoning.

9 Evenly divide the vegetables between 4 hot soup plates and arrange a selection of seafood on each. Spoon the reduced cooking liquid over and sprinkle with chervil. Serve with Melba toast on the side.

MELBA TOAST

MAKES 12 SLICES
6 slices white bread

1 Preheat the grill. Toast the bread on both sides under the grill until crisp and golden.
Use a bread knife to cut off the crusts, then horizontally slice each piece of bread into 2
slices: place the bread flat on the work surface with the palm of your hand on top and
slide the knife back and forth between your hand and the surface to cut 2 equal slices.
2 Cut each slice of bread in half diagonally, then return the bread to the grill,
untoasted side up. Continue toasting until golden brown and the ends curl. Wrap the
slices of Melba toast in a cloth and serve warm. Melba toast will, however, stay crisp
in an airtight container for a day and can be reheated in an 180°C/Gas 4 oven.

Stilton and Mixed Salad with Pears and Caramelised Pecans

SERVES 4

FOR THE STILTON AND PEAR SALAD:

2 perfectly fresh pears, such as a Comice

1 tablespoon freshly squeezed lemon juice

4 tablespoons vinaigrette dressing (see Basics, page 99)

4 handfuls mixed salad leaves, such as escarole curly endive, radicchio and mâche

50 g Stilton cheese

FOR THE CARAMELISED PECANS:

Sunflower oil

1 ½ tablespoons caster sugar

60 g pecan nuts

1 First, make the caramelised pecans. Lightly oil a baking sheet or marble slab and oil the tines of 2 metal forks.

2 Melt the sugar in a dry frying pan over a high heat, stirring just until it dissolves and forms a syrup. It is important the sugar dissolves before the syrup boils.

3 As soon as the syrup starts boiling, stop stirring. Leave the mixture to boil, using a wet pastry brush to wipe any splashes from the side of the pan, until a rich golden-brown caramel forms.

4 Stir in the pecans until they are coated, then immediately tip the nuts and caramel on to the baking sheet or marble slab and use the fork to separate the nuts; do not touch the hot caramel. Leave until cool and set, then coarsely chop the nuts.

5 Meanwhile, peel, core and chop the pears, dripping them into a bowl of water to stop them browning.

6 Pick over the salad leaves and rinse them well, then dry them completely in a tea towel. Put the salad dressing in a large bowl. Add the salad leaves and use your hands to toss together until all the leaves are lightly coated.

7 Drain the pears and dry them completely on a tea towel. Add the pears to the salad leaves, crumble in the blue cheese and toss again.

8 Separate the cool caramelised pecans and set aside.

9 To plate the salads, put a quarter of the salad mixture in a 10 cm wide bowl and place a serving plate, top-side down, on top. Make sure the bowl is in the centre of the plate, then invert the bowl and plate. Lift off the bowl, so the salad is slightly mounded. Sprinkle a quarter of the pecans over. Plate the remaining salads and serve.

Fresh and Smoked Haddock Serviche with Prawns on a Chiffonade of Radicchio

SERVES 6

400 g haddock fillet

200 g undyed smoked haddock fillet

200 g large raw prawns

2 large lemons

1 lime

2 tablespoons extra-virgin olive oil, not too strong

2 spring onions, finely chopped

Half a teaspoon coriander seeds, lightly crushed

1 teaspoon sea salt

A pinch of dried chilli flakes or cayenne pepper

TO SERVE:

2 heads radicchio

Fresh coriander leaves

1 To prepare the seafood, remove the skins from both haddock fillets, then cut the flesh into 1 cm pieces. Peel the prawns, discarding the heads and shells. Use a small knife to slice each prawn in half from head end to tail end, taking care to remove the black vein. Put all the seafood in a glass baking dish large enough to hold all the pieces in a single layer, then cover and place in the fridge.

2 Finely grate the rind from one lemon and the lime, and set aside. Roll the lemons firmly on the work surface, then cut in half and squeeze 100 ml juice. Cut the lime in half, squeeze 2 tablespoons juice and add to the lemon juice, along with the olive oil, spring onions, coriander seeds, salt and chilli. Stir together until the salt dissolves. Cover and chill until required.

3 About 1 ¼ hours before serving, pour the serviche mixture over the seafood and use your hands to mix together. Smooth the seafood pieces into a single layer again, re-cover the dish and return to the fridge for 1 hour, or until the plain haddock and prawn pieces appear white throughout.

4 Meanwhile, remove the radicchio leaves from the core, rinse well and pat completely dry on a tea towel. Roll up the leaves tightly like a cigar, then cut very thinly crosswise to make a chiffonade. Finely chop the coriander leaves.

5 To plate, remove the seafood from the fridge about 10 minutes before serving. Equally divide the radicchio between 4 plates, spreading it out into flat layers. Add the reserved lemon and lime rinds to the marinated seafood, then divide it equally between the plates. Spoon the remaining service mixture over the plates and sprinkle with chopped coriander.

Goats' Cheese-stuffed Ravioli with Mediterranean Sauce and Basil Oil

SERVES 6; MAKES 10 RAVIOLI

FOR THE GOATS' CHEESE-STUFFED PASTA:

100 g 'oo' pasta flour, plus extra

¼ teaspoon salt

1 medium egg, beaten

1 teaspoon olive oil

About 300 g soft, full-flavoured goats' cheese, rind removed if necessary

Salt and pepper

Basil oil, see below

FOR THE MEDITERRANEAN SAUCE:

1 tablespoon olive oil

2 large shallots, finely chopped

1 garlic clove

400 g canned chopped tomatoes

Pinch of sugar

100g sweet red peppers preserved in oil, well drained

100 g black olives, such as Niçoise

2 tablespoons capers in brine

Salt and pepper

Passata, optional

1 The Mediterranean sauce can be made up to 2 days in advance for reheating just before serving. Heat the oil in a saucepan over a medium heat. Add the shallots and garlic and stir for 3 to 5 minutes until the shallots are soft. Add the tomatoes and their juices, sugar and salt and pepper to taste. Bring to the boil, stirring, then leave to simmer over very low heat, partially covered, stirring frequently, until the liquid evaporates.

2 Meanwhile, cut the red peppers into 5 mm strips, then into dice. Pit and cut the olives into 5 mm dice. Drain and rinse the capers, then very coarsely chop. Set these aside.

3 Transfer the sauce to a blender and blitz until smooth, then rub through a fine sieve. Stir in the red pepper, olive and capers, then taste and adjust the seasoning, if necessary. Leave to cool completely and cover and chill until required.

4 To make the pasta dough, sift the flour and salt into a large bowl. Make a well in the centre and add the egg and oil. Use a fork to slowly mix the flour into the eggs until the liquid is absorbed, adding a few drops of water if necessary. Knead the dough on a very lightly floured work surface until it is smooth and elastic, about 10 minutes. Wrap the dough in clingfilm and leave to rest for 30 minutes.

5 Cut the dough into 2 equal pieces, then roll it out, using a pasta machine and following the manufacturer's instructions until the pasta is as thin as 2 sheets of paper stacked together.

6 Using an 8.5 cm round cutter, stamp out 20 discs. Cover with another tea towel and set aside.

7 Put the goats' cheese in a bowl and use a fork to beat until smooth. Different goats' cheeses have differing degrees of saltiness and flavour, so taste and add pepper and salt, if necessary.

8 Lay 10 dough discs on the work surface. Equally divide the goats' cheese between the centre of each disc. Using a pastry brush, 'paint' water around the edge of each disc, then top with the remaining discs. Use your fingers to firmly press the discs together to seal.

9 Meanwhile, bring a large pan of salted water to the oil. Transfer the sauce to a saucepan and bring to the boil. Reduce the heat and simmer, watching so it doesn't burn. Add a little passata or water if it becomes too thick.

10 Add 6 of the stuffed ravioli to the boiling water and continue boiling for 5 minutes, stirring gently occasionally so the pasta cooks evenly. (The remaining raviolis can be covered with clingfilm and chilled for up to 2 days before boiling.)

11 Divide the sauce between 6 hot soup plates. Very carefully drain the ravioli in a colander, then use a slotted spoon to transfer a raviolo to each of the bowls, shaking off any excess water. Drizzle blobs of basil oil over each raviolo and the sauce. Serve at once.

BASIL OIL

MAKES ABOUT 75 ML

30 g fresh basil leaves and stems

90 g olive oil

1 Blanch the basil leaves in a pan of boiling water for 15 seconds, then drain well and immediately plunge them into a bowl of ice water to stop the cooking and set the colour. Drain the basil and pat it completely dry with kitchen paper; transfer it to a small food processor or blender.

2 Heat the olive oil just until small bubbles appear; do not boil. Pour the warm oil over the basil and blitz until the leaves and stems are chopped. Scrape the oil and basil into a small bowl, cover tightly with clingfilm and leave to infuse for at least 2 hours.

3 Set a fine sieve over a bowl and add the oil and basil. Leave the oil to drip, without pressing, for an hour, shaking the strainer occasionally. Transfer to an airtight container and store at room temperature.

STARTERS

Preparing Shellfish

Fresh shellfish is always popular for starters. Whatever the recipe, they are all prepared in the same way to extract the flesh and deal with the shells, etc.

Crab

When buying live crabs, it's best to make sure they are lively characters; this ensures their freshness with that maximum flavour. Court bouillon or water can be used to boil the crabs. If working with water, add 50 g sea salt to every 2.25 litres. This proportion re-creates the taste of sea salt, resulting in very flavoursome crabmeat, full of natural sweetness.

To kill the crab, pierce the nerves set between and behind the eyes using a large skewer. Then weigh it and plunge into the boiling liquor. Return to a boil, then time according to the weight:
a 500 g crab will need just 15 minutes
a 1 kg crab – 20 minutes
a 1.5 kg crab – 25 minutes
larger crabs will need up to 30 minutes

Once cooked, remove from the water and leave to cool.

Crabs can also be cooked without prekilling, starting the process in cold salted water or court bouillon. As they are gradually brought to the boil they will drown. If following this method, remove 5 minutes from each cooking time, leaving the crabs to cool in the liquor.

Here's a step-by-step guide when removing the meat from cooked crab:

Lay the crab back shell down, breaking off the claws, along with the legs, removing their knuckle joint too.

The tail flap connected to the body can now be pulled back and snapped off.

To remove the body, insert the blade of a large thick knife between the body and the back shell, twisting to release. The body will now lever away from the shell, removing it completely.

On the body, you will find grey, feathery-like gills. These are known as 'dead man's fingers'; these pull away easily and can be discarded.

Place the shell on a board with the eyes facing you and press on the small piece of shell still attached, snapping it away easily, then remove the intestines and stomach sac.

Any brown meat left in the shell can be scooped into a bowl, keeping it separate from any white crab flakes.

Spoon any brown meat sitting in the centre of the body, adding it to that from the shell.

Cut the body section in half, revealing any white meat set within the crevices. This can be loosened and removed using a skewer or crab pick. This can be continued, cutting each half once more, cracking the shell each time a new cavity is found.

Crack open the claws with the back of a knife or small hammer. The meat can now easily be removed, releasing the flesh from the thin pieces of bone set in the pincers.

The legs can also be snapped or cracked open, scooping any meat free with a skewer or crab pick.

The white meat is best checked through for any shell splinters. The best way of doing this is to check with the tip of a fork as you shred the flesh. The brown meat varies – sometimes thick and firm, other times quite runny. For a smooth finish, push the brown meat through a sieve, or simply roughly chop for a chunky texture.

Traditional accompaniments, in particular for dressed crab, are chopped hard-boiled egg yolks and white, along with chopped parsley. A spoonful or two of mayonnaise bound with the brown crabmeat creates a nice spreading consistency, ready for warm toasts, or just brown bread and butter.

A 1 kg crab will normally provide you with about 350 g of white and brown crabmeat.

Crab and Chicory Salad

SERVES 4
1 head chicory, broken into leaves
1 head baby gem lettuce
½ cucumber, halved and thinly sliced
250 g white crabmeat, flaked
1 lime, cut into wedges
Sea salt and freshly ground black pepper
FOR THE DRESSING:
2 teaspoons fresh grated ginger
1 clove garlic, crushed
Grated zest and juice of 1 large lime
4 tablespoons vinaigrette (see Basics, page 99)
½ teaspoon caster sugar
4 to 6 large leaves fresh mint, shredded
2 spring onions, chopped
1 fresh red chilli, seeded and chopped, optional

1 Line 4 shallow sundae glasses with the larger chicory leaves. Shred the smaller ones along with the lettuce and mix with the cucumber. Scatter in the bases of the dishes.
2 Mix together the dressing ingredients, adding chilli if you like a bit of a bite. Stir into the flaked crab then spoon on top of the lettuce. Serve lightly chilled, garnished with a lime wedge.

Lobster

There are several ways of preparing and cooking lobster. It is best to cook them fresh and alive. But if the thought of killing a lobster is off-putting, the calmest way is to freeze them, still alive, for 2 hours. This renders them relaxed in a state of hibernation ready to be prepared.

To cook – Method A
→ Boil a large pan of well-salted water, dropping in the 'pre-frozen' (see above) lobsters.
→ Once returned to the boil, cook 450 g to 750 g sizes for 8 to 10 minutes, then remove and leave until cool enough to handle. For anything larger, up to 1.2 kg lobsters, allow 15 minutes of boiling

To cook – Method B
→ The court bouillon is a classic cooking liquor in which to cook shellfish. Bring a large pan of water to the boil and add the juice of 2 lemons, plus bay leaves and sprigs of dill, thyme and parsley and 1 teaspoon of peppercorns, toughly crushed and tied in a muslin bag.
→ Boil the court bouillon in a large saucepan. Drop the lobsters in the liquor, cooking for just a few minutes. Remove the pan from the heat, allowing the lobsters to remain in the liquor for 10 to 15 minutes or until completely cold, before removing the meat from the shell.
→ To remove meat from a cooked lobster, remove the large claws and use a nutcracker or a small hammer to crack the shells, then remove the meat from the claws. Next, hold the lobster in one hand and use your other hand to break the tail from the body.
→ Use kitchen shears or a knife to slice through the soft shell on the underside of the lobster and use your fingers to prise out the tail meat. The claw and tail meat are the most tender and flavoursome, but there is also more meat in the lobster's body, which you can extract by holding the body, eyes downward, and pulling the upper body shell apart. You will find the meat between the cartilage.

Cooked Lobster for grilling in the shell:

→ Lay the cooked lobster on a chopping board. Cut in half lengthways, first through

→ the middle of the head between the eyes, before turning and repeating through the centre of the tail.

→ Remove and discard the black intestinal tract set in the tail, along with the stomach sac found in the head section of each half. Note: the red roe (when raw – green coral) and greenish tomalley (liver) can be left in, or removed; if removed, stir them into warm sauces, to be served with the dish for extra flavour. They add a vibrant pink colour to sauces, risottos, etc.

→ Crack the claws with the back of a heavy knife. These can be left attached, particularly if grilling on the barbecue. For finishing under a preheated grill, remove the lobster meat from the claws, leaving in large pieces or dicing, arranging them in the head cavity of each half.

→ The lobster is now ready for grilling, roasting or dicing for stews, casseroles or salads.

Note: it's not essential to halve the lobsters before removing from the shell. The claws and tail can be pulled away from the head. To remove the claw meat, proceed as above. For the tail, holding the firm shell in the palm of your hand, cut along either side of the more translucent underside, pulling it back before lifting the tail free. To remove the black intestinal tract, simply make a small incision along the centre of the tail, pulling it away in one piece and discarding.

Raw lobster for grilling:

→ Put the lobster in the freezer for two hours as described above in the introduction.

→ Cut and split the lobster in two down the centre, creating two equal halves.

→ Remove and discard the stomach sac (this is slightly clear in colour, and split between both heads), along with the intestinal tract that runs through the tail.

→ The greenish tomalley (liver) and green coral (roe) can be left in, both offering extra flavour to the lobster.

→ Crack the claws with a heavy knife and the lobsters are ready to grill.

Note: a translucent bone is set in the main large claw of the lobster. Once cooked, this can be pulled away quite easily, first pulling away the small pincer before following with the bone. Halved lobster can also be blanched in boiling salted water for just a minute or two, then removed; when cool enough to handle, the meat can be pulled away. This method is not often used, but is ideal for adding lobster to fish casseroles, stews or steaming for warm salads.

Oysters

How to open oysters:

→ Using a thick cloth or folded tea towel, hold the oyster flat-side uppermost. Push a stubby sharp knife into the hinge situated at the narrowest point of the shell.

→ Applying forceful pressure, move the knife back and forth, twisting to release the hinge. You will feel the muscle suddenly give.

→ Gently lift the lid off the shell, cutting away the muscle connecting the flesh to the shell. Keeping the bottom upright and, saving the juices in the shell, the oyster can be released, loosening it from the base with the knife.

→ Pick out any loose splinters from the shell and juice before serving.

→ Best served on a bed of crushed ice with wedges of fresh lemon and a small bottle of Tabasco sauce to shake cautious dashes onto the flesh.

Squid

There are two main parts to the squid, the head and tentacles, and the main body sac. Larger squid can be cut into rings, squares or strips. Alternatively, leave the body sac whole (after thoroughly cleansing it) and stuff before roasting, poaching or grilling.

How to prepare a squid:

→ Hold the body sac with one hand and the tentacles and head with the other, and gently pull them away from the body. This also removes the milky white intestines from the body attached to them, and any left behind can be easily scooped out with a forefinger.

→ Separate the tentacles from the head, cutting them off just in front of the eyes, discarding the head. Squeeze out the small beak from the centre of the tentacles and discard.

→ If wishing to use the ink sac, this will be found among the intestines, a silvery-blue pouch ready to cut away. This has a deliciously sweet flavour and adds a great inky blue-grey to pasta and sauces.

→ Pull away the transparent quill from inside the body.

→ Cut or pull away the two fins, peeling off this purple-brown membrane-like skin from both the body and fins. (The fins can be kept and cooked or discarded as you please.)

→ The body can now be cut into rings, and if the tentacles are large they can be roughly chopped. But most of the time, they are left whole and curl attractively when cooked.

→ For pieces and strips, insert a sharp knife into the body, cutting open along one side.

→ Open the body flat, scraping away any traces of membrane or intestines.

→ Score the inner side with the tip of a sharp knife in a criss-cross pattern before cutting the squid into 5 cm pieces or strips. The squid is now ready for cooking.

1 CHEF IS A FOUR-LETTER WORD

'You are the actors, this is your stage …
it's important we don't lose our cool,
we work as a team, and we go for it.'

Jean-Christophe Novelli

It takes a certain kind of person to want to be part of Hell's Kitchen. The trainees need more than a passion for food. In the course of two trying weeks, they will also suffer relentless abuse, sleep deprivation, and separation from family and friends. They will have to be fearless, willing to pitch themselves into the melee of a professional kitchen, with no certainty of emerging again in one piece. Which begs the question why anyone in their right mind would choose to volunteer for such an ordeal? Put simply, there is a huge amount at stake; the opportunity to learn from a world-class chef, for starters and, for the winner, a grand prize of £250,000 and the chance to have a restaurant of their own. Whether anyone would still want to run a restaurant, of course, after a fortnight in Hell's Kitchen remained to be seen. Perhaps, after a bout of therapy.

As the trainees arrived in Hell's Kitchen, stepping out of a chauffeur-driven car onto a red carpet, maître d' Laura Vanninen welcomed them, and split them into blue and red teams. They sipped champagne, taking in the sumptuous surroundings of the restaurant, unaware that before they'd even finished their drinks they'd be heading into the kitchen to start work.

First to arrive at Hell's Kitchen was Stein Smart, 32, a burly builder from Essex, with ambitions to open a restaurant called Fat Blokes. 'I like giving people proper big portions,' he said. 'None of that *nouvelle cuisine* rubbish.' What Stein didn't know was that, as a member of the blue team, he would be working with Jean-Christophe Novelli.

'I'm loud, gobby, flash, confident,' said Stein, for the benefit of anyone not sure. 'I don't pull any punches. What you see is what you get.'

Next to arrive was Caroline Garvey, a 54-year-old company director, and the first member of the red team. With her cut-glass accent, impeccable manners and aristocratic air, she might have landed from another planet. Indeed, that was something Gary Rhodes would speculate about as the days wore on.

Next came Kellie Cresswell, from Kent. Kellie, 28, wide-eyed as she walked through the imposing entrance of Hell's Kitchen, would join the blue team. It was all a world away from her usual surroundings, working in a pub where, until recently, she had been scrubbing pots.

Simon Gross, 36, a waiter, the second member of the red team to bowl in, had already confessed to being 'the terriblest cook ever'. That was the last thing on his mind, though, as he swept through the restaurant. His face lit up. 'Wow, I like that chandelier. It would make a nice earring, wouldn't it?' he gushed. 'Champagne? I feel like royalty.'

Next came Aaron Siwoku, just 22 years old, but already an entrepreneur, and the third member of the red team. Smooth, suave, cool and confident, he gazed around the restaurant. In the mirrored walls, his reflection gazed back.

Terry Miller, a 46-year-old with a catering business in Newcastle, was the next red-team member to arrive. A giant Geordie whose accent would prove almost as difficult for the trainees to decipher as Jean-Christophe's, Terry was looking forward to some straightforward cooking, preferably English. 'The French, where you're putting all those little bits on, I'd be hopeless,' he said, shaking his head. 'I've got a touch like an elephant. Wye aye.'

Aby King, 28, and a PA from London, the next member of the blues to arrive, confessed to having a crush on Jean-Christophe Novelli. 'He is unbelievably sexy,' she said.

Joining Aby in the blue team was thirty-year-old Gary Tomlin, a chef in a Caribbean takeaway. For Gary, Hell's Kitchen represented catering heaven, and the answer to his prayers.

Last to arrive were single mum Sam Ramplin, 31, the final member of the red team, and law student Henry Filloux-Bennett, 22, the last of the blues. 'I'm arrogant,' he said,' but that's only because you have to have a little bit of self-confidence to get anywhere in life.'

In Hell's Kitchen, though, as Henry was about to find out, arrogance wouldn't get him very far.

So, ten trainees, all very different. Presenter Angus Deayton summed them up as, 'feisty, sexy, irritating, arrogant, pretty, posh, dull and stupid … almost everything except an accomplished cook'.

With the trainees still taking in their surroundings and getting to know their new team-mates, they were sent into the kitchen to prepare their signature dishes – intended to reflect the personality of their creator – for the chefs. They had 45 minutes. The niceties over, from now on they would be working.

In the red kitchen, as the trainees toiled over a variety of hot stoves, Adam Gray, sous chef to Gary Rhodes, chivvied them on. Keeping an eye on things in the blue kitchen was Chris Wheeler, a member of Jean-Christophe's trusted team. As both men egged on the trainees, signs of tension were already beginning to show.

In the blue kitchen, Gary, sweat running off his brow, struggled to open a jar. In the red kitchen, Simon whipped a pan of pasta off the stove as it boiled over. 'It's a complete and utter catastrophe,' he muttered.

'Guys, you must remember, this is the first impression,' said Adam Gray, surveying a scene bordering on chaos. 'This is the first thing the chef is going to see.'

Not that the trainees, at that stage, had any inkling which chef they were out to impress. As they lined up behind their finished dishes, a sense of apprehension hung in the air. Jean-Christophe and Gary Rhodes, their starchy expressions in keeping with their crisp chef's whites, swept into the kitchen. The ten trainees stood to attention, rigid with nerves, as their mentors looked them up and down. 'Oh God,' whispered Simon, screwing his eyes shut.

Finally, it was revealed which chef would be in charge of which team. A small cheer went up for Jean-Christophe from his trainees; a ripple of polite applause for Gary Rhodes. Everyone seemed pleased, although not for long. As soon as the chefs began tasting the signature dishes, anxiety took hold.

Jean-Christophe peered uncertainly at a dish. 'It's me, oh shit,' said Henry, stepping forwards.

'What is it?' said Jean-Christophe.

'Hopefully, a ravioli of langoustine and

lobster on sweet-potato croutons with truffle, spinach and lobster bisque,' said Henry, with the look of someone hoping the ground would open up and swallow him.

Jean-Christophe took a tentative mouthful. 'Ooh,' he said, reaching for some water. 'Stick your finger in the sauce and tell me how it tastes.'

As Henry pronounced the sauce 'rough', Jean-Christophe glared at him. 'If it's rough, why did you do it?'

Henry had tried his best but it was far from good enough. 'I was gutted,' he said. 'To be told your food is rough is a bit of a letdown.' A bad start, then, but things would soon get a lot worse for the hapless student.

Things weren't much better in the red kitchen as Aaron presented his offering of pan-fried sea bass and pesto mash to his head chef. 'Is there something raw about your personality?' Gary Rhodes wondered, wafting a floret of uncooked broccoli at him.

The potato, however, saved the entrepreneur. 'You made this mash?' said the chef. 'There's hope, Aaron. This is a disaster, but there's something there.'

Stein had prepared paella. Jean-Christophe pronounced the rice overcooked and the prawns undercooked. The seasoning, however, was perfect.

In the red kitchen, Caroline, delighted to be in the Rhodes team, stepped forwards to hear the verdict on her pork fillet cooked with herbs. In her enthusiasm to greet the chef, she made the fatal error of using a four-letter word; an innocent enough mistake since Gary is, after all, his name.

'What did you call me?' the chef demanded, infuriated.

Wisely, Caroline decided to keep quiet. 'I didn't,' she said.

'My name is *chef*,' he said.

As for her signature dish, Caroline expressed concern it was overcooked. Gary Rhodes was dismissive. 'I think it's totally ruined,' he said.

In the background, Simon had his head

in his hands, but Caroline was undeterred, insisting that she liked Gary's – or, rather, *chef's* – no-nonsense approach. 'I think we all enjoy discipline,' she said.

Jean-Christophe found merit in Kellie's salmon dish. 'It's not the best thing to happen to me, but it's good,' he told her.

Simon, however, was in for a savaging over his spaghetti bolognese. '*That's* spaghetti bolognese?' asked Gary, poking it with a fork.

'It's my interpretation,' Simon said.

'Is it going to excite my palate?'

'Probably not, chef.'

He was right. 'Do you really think anyone could sit down and eat a plate of that?' asked the chef. 'I think we've got a lot of work to do.' What Gary didn't know was quite how much work he would have to do with Simon, whose knowledge of food was less than basic.

In the blue kitchen, Aby stepped forwards to hear what Jean-Christophe had to say about the signature dish she had named Sexy Chicken. Not much, it transpired. 'You think this is sexy?' he said. 'Bloody hell, this is rough.'

It was not the first impression Aby had hoped for. 'It's a dish I made up,' she said. 'Clearly it was a huge mistake to present it to the utterly, utterly gorgeous Novelli.'

As Sam presented her signature dish to Gary Rhodes nerves got the better of her. 'It's shit–' she stuttered, 'shit– I can't say it,' she said, tripping over the name of the mushrooms she had used in her stir-fry.

'Shitake,' he told her, tasting it. 'There are elements to this cooking that has hope,' he said, causing Sam to sigh with relief.

Jean-Christophe turned his attention to his final trainee's dish. Gary had prepared jerk chicken with fried dumplings, Caribbean style. The chef pulled a face, chewing on a dumpling. 'For fifteen days, my friend, listen to every single tip I give you,' said Jean-Christophe. 'This is not right.'

Finally, in the red kitchen, Terry stepped forwards with a dish he had named King Prawn Rockefeller: prawns with a potato topping on a bed of spinach. The trainee admitted he had taken a short cut and used instant potato. Gary stared at him in disbelief. 'Here you are trying to impress a professional chef with instant mashed potato. Not a good start, is it?'

'No, I've made a right arse of meself,' Terry said.

It has taken both chefs a matter of seconds to get the measure of their teams and it is not encouraging. In just a few hours the first diners will arrive at Hell's Kitchen, where both teams are facing a language barrier. In the blue kitchen, the trainees are struggling with the accent of their chef. In the red kitchen, Geordie Terry battles to make himself understood, already feeling as if he is the outsider of the group. A North–South divide appears to be developing. The fact that Aaron is from Cheshire – technically in the Northwest – is of little consolation.

'I wonder if they'll bring in a Geordie interpretater (sic),' muses Terry.

In the blue kitchen, the team runs through their menu in a state of mild shock. Some of the dishes are so complicated it takes a couple of lines to describe them. The trainees are nonplussed. The efforts of their head chef to translate aren't doing much to allay their fears.

'I can't understand a word he's saying,' says Stein.

Gary agrees. 'His accent is double hard,' he says.

Jean-Christophe makes no concessions. 'Every time I say something to you I'm going to ask a question and you better respond clearly,' he tells them. 'Memorise everything I say to you or I'm going to ask you to do the washing up for fifteen minutes. Is it clear?'

It's not, but they nod anyway.

In the red kitchen, as the trainees prepare for the first night's service in the restaurant, Gary Rhodes begins to appreciate the enormity of the task facing him. He catches Simon holding a knife upside down, trying to cut with the blunt side of the blade. None of the trainees knows how to poach an egg, one

of the ingredients for his English breakfast salad starter. 'This is driving me nuts already,' says Gary, his voice showing early signs of strain from shouting at his team. 'Don't make me shout and scream,' he croaks at them.

Just when it seems things can't get any worse, Simon reveals he doesn't know the difference between a whisk and a spatula. He doesn't know which bit of an egg is the yolk either although, luckily, as service approaches, he manages to keep that to himself.

With just minutes to go before the first diners arrive, both chefs try to rally their teams. 'You are the actors, this is your stage. I don't want no one to panic,' says Jean-Christophe. 'It's important we don't lose our cool, we work as a team, and we go for it.' Words that will return to haunt him as the night wears on.

As the restaurant fills up, both kitchens wait for their first check to come in. It goes to the blues, much to their delight. They're off. In the red kitchen, frustration mounts as the minutes tick by and checks continue to arrive at the blue-kitchen pass. An hour after service has begun, the reds get their first check.

In both kitchens the evening has begun in an atmosphere of relative calm, so much so that Jean-Christophe leaves the pass to greet guests. Among those in the restaurant is the celebrated – and prophetic, it turns out – chef, Keith Floyd. As if sensing the furious outburst that will soon send shock waves through the blue kitchen, he says, 'Jean-Christophe is a great leader but don't forget he *is* French, and *de temps en temps il va explosé.*' (From time to time he is going to explode.)

Jean-Christophe, however, is keen to keep a cool head. 'Just be yourself, have confidence, allow yourself to f**k up,' he tells his team. 'I'm not going to scream. I will only lose it if you're not listening.'

In the red kitchen, initially Gary Rhodes is pleased with the quality of the food coming to the pass. 'If you continue giving me food like this you're going to make me happy,' he says. Before long, though, as standards slip,

his mood changes. 'How can I serve that?' he demands. 'Chuck it out.' He turns to Aaron. 'Don't slam things round in my kitchen. Treat them with respect. Do as the head chef says. *Full stop.*'

Meanwhile, actress Daniella Westbrook has found a stray piece of tin foil in her goats' cheese starter. Maître d' Laura takes it back to Jean-Christophe.

In the red kitchen, Gary Rhodes has reached the end of his tether. He decides to close the kitchen. 'It's not good enough,' he tells the trainees. 'I'm not putting my reputation on the line.' Two hungry diners approach the pass, pleading for food, but Gary is resolute. He will not serve second-rate nosh.

Meanwhile, things are reaching boiling point in the blue kitchen where Henry has managed to infuriate Jean-Christophe by bringing a cold goats' cheese starter to the pass. He is also struggling with the mushroom pancake. 'I can't remember how to do it,' he says. 'It's a joke,' the chef tells him, not smiling.

When Henry pours a beef sauce on the mushrooms – a vegetarian starter – it is the final straw. Jean-Christophe slams the plate against the wall. 'Get out of the kitchen, get the f**k out of here,' he yells. As Henry leaves, his chef whacks a rack of serving spoons suspended from the ceiling. They rain down on the retreating trainee as the rest of the blue team look on, shocked.

Outside, Henry sits with his head in his hands while, in the kitchen, a porter patiently replaces the scattered utensils in their rack. Stein is outraged. 'If that had have been me I'd have thrown them back at him,' he says.

Blue trainee Gary decides to give Jean-Christophe a wide berth. 'The chef's like a madman,' he says.

Henry, whose dreams of running his own restaurant are fading fast, feels his chef has gone too far. 'What he did was absolutely ridiculous because it did nothing but harm our morale and my self-esteem,' he says.

Jean-Christophe takes a different view,

however. 'I didn't think he had the right attitude, simple as that.'

At the end of the first night's service, the diners' verdicts are delivered to each chef.

Gary Rhodes, having closed his kitchen early, scores a dismal two and a half points out of ten. The news is greeted with silence by a tired, disheartened red team. 'There are huge lessons to be learned,' Gary says. 'We weren't up to standard. The red team failed.'

In the blue kitchen, the news they have scored five out of ten, trouncing their rivals, brings cheers. As the reality of running a top-class kitchen starts to sink in, Kellie says, 'Has anybody had second thoughts about actually owning their own restaurant?'

Already, the first sacking from Hell's Kitchen is looming and the chefs must nominate the weakest member of their team for the public to vote on. Gary Rhodes, his voice hoarse, picks Simon who, despite having spent much of his first day in the kitchen being berated by the chef, appears shocked. Jean-Christophe nominates Henry, the trainee whose failings had prompted a plate-smashing, spoon-throwing episode.

No surprises there, then.

The following morning, after barely four hours' sleep, the trainees are back in the kitchen, bleary-eyed, for roll call. As the reds line up, a grim-looking Gary Rhodes faces them.

He tackles Aaron about his attitude the night before during service. 'You stood there, you stared at me on the hot plate because I had to bawl you out a couple of times. You didn't like it.'

Aaron makes the fatal mistake of answering back. 'I think please and thank you and a little bit of encouragement would go a long way,' he says.

All Gary wants to hear, however, is *Yes, chef*. 'I haven't got time for *Thank you, pleasey pleasey, nicey nicey,*' he says. 'I call, you say – "Yes, chef!"'

Gary is after perfection and there is a long way to go. He sends the trainees back into the kitchen to work on getting the menu up to scratch. As the red kitchen starts work, Gary keeps an eye on Simon. 'He does not listen to the most basic and simple of orders,' the chef complains. 'He's "*Yes, chef, Yes, chef,*" but he's not taking any of it in.'

Simon, meanwhile, is feeling the pressure. 'Having somebody on your back all the time when your intentions are good and you are trying can actually make you fail,' he says.

Gary, though, is determined to prove to Simon that he can cook if he puts his mind to it. He shows him how to pan-fry fish to perfection. Gary says, 'How does that look? Nice?'

'Excellent, chef,' Simon agrees.

'And who made it?'

'You,' says Simon.

Gary shakes his head. '*You*. That's how you're going to cook it tonight, aren't you?'

'I am, chef.'

As Hell's Kitchen opens again, Gary Rhodes is determined to have a better night. His team is right behind him.

Simon, despite having been on the receiving end of much of Gary's rage on Day One, and facing the sack, remains upbeat, no doubt buoyed by having cooked the perfect fish under the chef's watchful eye. 'I'm a lot more confident and really full of energy and zest,' he says. 'I really want it to be a smooth night for everybody and I'm raring to go.'

Among the first guests to arrive is weathergirl Sian Lloyd, who's given a table with a good view of both kitchens. Jean-Christophe spots her and goes out to say hello. She and her dining companion are treated to a Novelli kiss.

Jean-Christophe returns to the blue pass, confident of their order. Within seconds,

though, Gary Rhodes is at their table. Sian tells him that his rival has already been out, doing his best to sway their allegiance with a kiss. 'We're not easily bought,' she says, assuring him that she and her friend will be ordering from the red kitchen. 'We're Gary's girls,' she adds, laughing.

Gary is delighted. 'It just goes to show he doesn't kiss very well.'

The second night belongs to the red team, with a respectable six and a half out of ten. It's level pegging.

Jean-Christophe is infuriated by the diners' verdict, in particular the comment from one person on the blue menu's *late season wild mushrooms wrapped in a thin poppy seed pancake, melted foie gras vintage parmesan crackling* starter. He reads aloud in disbelief. 'Mushroom starter – too many mushrooms. Who the f**k do they think they are?' he says.

At the end of the evening, either Simon or Henry will go. Viewers have been casting their votes since the nominations were announced the night before. As the pair wait for Angus Deayton to deliver the verdict, Simon is confident. As for Henry, despite having a canteen of catering spoons dropped on him from a height, he insists it's all going 'awesomely well'.

Seconds later, Angus Deayton breaks the news that Henry will be leaving. Simon returns to the red kitchen, triumphant.

With the scores even, the reds now have one more trainee in the kitchen than their rivals; an advantage, surely. In a conventional kitchen, perhaps, but in the pressure cooker that is Hell's Kitchen – where learning to duck flying utensils is as crucial as knowing when a steak is medium rare – no one is taking bets.

2 FALLING OUT . . . AND FALLING FOR EACH OTHER

'I want perfection – only perfection.
It's all I expect to see.' Gary Rhodes

After another night of too-little sleep, the red team reassembles. Despite their win the night before, there's no room for complacency, yet there's an air of sloppiness about the trainees that rankles Gary Rhodes. He casts a critical eye over his team. Aaron, who should know better by now, hasn't bothered with his chef's hat.

'I know you're a big, tall, hunky, good-looking guy – sexiest man in the world,' Gary says, 'but I don't want you to be the sexiest man in the world, I want you to be a better cook.'

Simon, still deflated from his near-sacking experience, knows he must do better if he's to impress his chef. He feels like the dunce of the team, and it's affecting his confidence. He's not the only one causing concern, though. Big Terry – singled out by the chef as the strongest trainee – had performed poorly during service. Gary urges him to raise his game.

Just a few days in, and Hell's Kitchen appears to be taking its toll on Sam and, in particular, Caroline. 'You have got to look at yourselves as winners,' Gary says.

'You have your reputation, I have my reputation,' Caroline says. 'I know I'm a good cook. I wish to prove it for a few more days.' It's just the kind of fighting talk Gary likes although, as Caroline will discover as the day wears on, he expects

it to be matched by performance.

In the blue kitchen, Jean-Christophe awaits his team, disappointed at having lost out to the reds the previous night. His troops, however, are upbeat. They think they did a good job. Stein believes they had a good service. 'We know what we're doing,' he says. 'I'm disheartened with the verdict.'

Kellie agrees. 'It was a fantastic night, whether we won or not.'

Aby, too, is getting to grips with the difficult task of preparing complicated desserts. Jean-Christophe, however, is not impressed with her working environment. In short, it's a tip. 'Start cleaning your space. If it's clean, your brain is clean,' he tells her. It's a ticking-off in anyone's language but Aby, still besotted with her French mentor, doesn't mind. At least he's speaking to her. It's when he's not that sparks start to fly.

Jean-Christophe believes what let the team down the night before was their presentation. Earlier, both chefs had set their teams a simple task – to decorate a chocolate pudding. It was an opportunity to use their imagination. In the red kitchen, Simon, having been battered by Gary, was out to impress.

In the blue kitchen, it was a chance for Aby to apply the knowledge she had gained on desserts. In theory, she should have wiped the floor with her team-

mates. And, if only she had stuck to the rules, she might have.

As Jean-Christophe inspected his trainees' efforts he was full of praise for everyone. Everyone but Aby, that is. Gary's dish was deemed 'very expressive, very versatile'. Aby, though, had messed up. Jean-Christophe regarded her dish with suspicion. 'Is that ice cream?' he said. She nodded. 'It is against the rules,' he said. To add to her misery, he invited the loser to step forwards. Aby, head bowed in shame, obliged. 'Thank you for being honest,' he said, as she dabbed at her tears with a tea towel.

'It's upsetting,' she said later. 'I swore I wouldn't cry.'

In the red kitchen, Simon is also upset. Gary Rhodes has given his team clear instructions about making their chocolate puddings appetising. 'It's all about presentation,' he says. 'The moment you see it, it appeals to the palate and you want to eat it.'

Simon, though, hasn't quite got the hang of what makes an edible dessert. As Gary fixes his dish with a look of disgust, Simon blurts out, 'It's disastrous.' Gary agrees.

'Strawberries all around the border. Why, what for?' the chef says.

Simon says, 'I've overdone it. I tried to go for something I could do.'

Sam's is the most impressive. Gary sums up her efforts as, 'exciting, colourful and neat'.

Caroline, however, fails. She has drenched her plate in cocoa powder. 'If that was presented to me I wouldn't want to eat it,' Gary tells her.

He turns to Simon. 'Yours is the losing dish.'

'Tell me why, so I can get it right next time,' says Simon.

'Your plate isn't even clean. It's disgustingly filthy with smudges all around, which is just not acceptable,' Gary tells him.

It is dawning on both head chefs that their teams are lacking in many of the fundamental skills needed to turn out first-rate food. They set to work to plug some of the gaps. For Jean-Christophe, this means schooling his trainees in the art of picking up a bottle of oil, pouring some in a pan, and replacing the bottle. Simple, *n'est ce pas? Non*.

The trainees watch, bemused, as their chef demonstrates, deftly grabbing the bottle, raising it in the air, expertly pouring just the right amount of oil into the pan, and replacing the bottle exactly where he found it. Bing, bang, boom. 'It's like any business. When you run a restaurant you've got to be fit,' says the chef.

Stein just about masters the technique but Gary struggles. 'My hands are big. This is very hard for me,' he says, taking himself off into a quiet corner to practise. After several attempts, the penny finally drops. 'The bottle has to be dry,' he concludes, to no one in particular. 'That's what it is, you know. Yeah, definitely – a dry bottle.'

In the red kitchen, Simon is also struggling with a job that at first sight appears utterly straightforward. He's preparing one of the desserts: crisp, thin apple tart with Bramley apple sorbet. All he has to do is cut up the apples, but he's making a mess of it. Gary Rhodes – perfectionist that he is – takes him to task.

'Who cut that apple?' he asks. Simon owns up. 'Repeat after me, I am stupid.' Simon swallows. 'I am stupid,' he says.

He starts again, muttering to himself. His next attempt also falls foul of his chef. 'Don't waste any sugar on that – show me first,' he says. Simon presents his apple segments. 'In the bin,' Gary tells him.

On current showing, Gary Rhodes is not convinced all of his trainees have sufficient dedication and energy to run a restaurant. Already, Sam, Simon and Caroline are wilting. 'You have to stay one hundred per cent in control and you have to keep your energy level high,' he says.

Terry, used to coping with the harsh conditions of the North, puts it more bluntly. 'I've never come across such a bunch of nancies in all me life,' he says. 'They're soft as shite down here.'

As the third service nears, the red kitchen is still not ready. 'If you're not ready, you fail,' Gary tells them. 'It's not good enough.' Caroline is far too cheerful for his liking. 'No time for smiling, Caroline,' he says.

In the blue kitchen, Jean-Christophe causes mild pandemonium by telling his team they will be swapping round and taking on new and unfamiliar tasks. Stein's jaw drops open while Gary frantically searches for a pen to take notes.

'He's really dropped us in the shit,' says Stein, perhaps concerned that he may be the next trainee to have a tray of cutlery land on him.

Despite his team's win the night before, Gary Rhodes is in no mood to take things easy. 'Anything that's slightly substandard – *anything* – is coming back,' he says. 'Tonight I want perfection only. Full stop. *Perfection.* It's all I expect to see. I don't care if I only feed ten people.'

Unfortunately, the team seems fresh out of perfection and as the checks begin to pour in, the trainees start to lose it. Big Terry – not so long ago, Gary's Number One – can't seem to get his steaks right. The fact he's burned a few is bad enough. Worse, he seems to find it funny.

'Get your act together,' Gary tells him.

Having demanded perfection, he finds himself sending dishes back. Steak. Overcooked. Salmon. Overcooked.

In the blue kitchen, Jean-Christophe's decision to assign his team new tasks is paying off. The atmosphere is calm. Stein, thrown in at the deep end on the meat dishes, is doing well. 'I love this place,' he says. 'It's just getting better and better. If I get voted off I'm going to chain myself to a lampshade or something. I am not moving.'

The blue team's efforts are getting mixed reactions in the restaurant. TV presenter Anna Walker is effusive about her starter. 'I had the goats' cheese, which was delicious,' she said, 'just what you want from a starter. Just right to get the taste buds going.

There's a thumbs down, though, from Timmy Mallett, who says, 'The real delight of the food was drowned out by the stuff on top. It's a bit of a shame.'

For the reds, Aaron finally manages to produce a salmon that Gary is happy to serve. Just as well, since most of the restaurant seems to want to order from the Rhodes menu.

Maître d' Laura, can sense tension building in the red kitchen. 'Tonight, Gary's kitchen has been incredibly popular and he's just got checks piling up on his pass, and I don't think he's got much hope of serving all that food,' she says.

Gary, meanwhile, barks orders at his team. 'Two scallops and a bass next away.' Silence. 'Caroline! Answer, me, goddammit! I am sick and tired of it. You have got to move at some pace.'

Big Terry is off form too. When he brings two charred steaks that were meant to be medium, Gary despairs. 'That's not medium.'

'Bit longer, chef?' Terry says helpfully.

'Don't mess around. You think that needs *longer*? It's medium well. It's overcooked. Don't serve it. Take it back. I'm not serving second-rate rubbish. It all goes back.'

In the restaurant, the diners who have chosen from the Rhodes menu are starting to wonder when – or if – they will actually get any food. Meanwhile, the wine continues to flow. Tennis player Annabel Croft has nibbled on a bread roll and a few pretzels, washed down with a lot of red – or is it white? – wine. After a two-hour wait, she's not sure.

In the red kitchen, Gary is fast losing his patience and, for once, it's not Simon in the firing line; suddenly Caroline can't do anything right. 'It absolutely drives me insane and in fact I want to start punching my own head in, screaming and beating myself up because it's driving me mad. Then I want to blame them for the bruises,' says Gary.

To make matters worse, Annabel Croft, by now practically faint with hunger, comes to the pass to beg for food. Gary tells her, 'The starters are coming. You'll get something to eat and that's a promise.' He shakes his head

in despair. 'This is embarrassing me tonight.'

Caroline – the cause of much of his embarrassment – has every sympathy. 'Poor chef went nuts,' she says. 'We all did. I'm here to help him win. If that means he has to scream at me in frustration, so be it.'

The harmonious atmosphere of the blue kitchen is also beginning to break down. Aby, slaving away over desserts, needs some assistance and Kellie finds herself running about, cleaning up after her team-mate. She is far from happy to be relegated to the role of glorified skivvy. 'I don't mind when people say please and thank you,' she says. 'It costs nothing. If it's a big chef, you do it, but not when somebody's the same level.'

When the diners' verdict comes in, it's another win for the blue kitchen. 'It's overwhelming, we did it again,' Jean-Christophe tells his delighted team. 'I cannot even sleep, I am so excited.'

The blue trainees are on a high. 'I've never been in a kitchen before,' says Stein, 'but now I'm getting into my stride and enjoying every moment.'

Rasta Gary admits to being tired and stressed. 'I didn't know it would be so hard, but I'm not giving up,' he says. 'You have to be a lion, a tiger – it's like the jungle. Be strong.'

'Whatever happens, I've got so much respect for Jean-Christophe,' says Stein. 'He's a diamond geezer.'

Aby has more than respect for her mentor. 'I'm so in love with him,' she says. 'I gush whenever he's near me.'

Within the space of a few hours, however, there will be little love lost between the two of them.

It's the morning after the night before and Caroline, still red-eyed, presents herself for roll call in dark glasses.

A grim-faced Gary surveys his team. 'I went home really sad and upset last night,' he says. 'I don't actually like shouting at my squad. I feel I have beaten you all up a little bit and it's not my style. I'm going to change the team

around and I'm going to be changing the menu.'

The red kitchen still has the edge with a full complement of chefs. With the odds in his favour, Gary is not prepared to suffer another defeat, even if it kills him. Or, more likely, one of his team.

In the blue kitchen, Jean-Christophe's team is upbeat. He's impressed with their performance the night before, particularly as he unsettled them just as service was about to start. 'When I gave you the good news about swapping dishes . . . your faces were a picture,' he says.

As he briefs his team, Aby's face remains a picture – a picture of longing for her head chef. The trainees set to work, but the harmonious mood of the kitchen is about to be upset. What Jean-Christophe doesn't know is that Aby is feeling slighted. It's bad enough that she thinks the chef is ignoring her but, to make matters worse, he doesn't seem to know her name. Aby can barely contain herself. She picks a fight in full view of everyone. On reflection, not the best way to win over the chef.

'I can't work if I am constantly being bashed,' she complains.

'You're making a scene now, just stop. What would you like to say?'

Fighting back tears, Aby tries to speak. 'Every time I say something to you, you blank me.'

Jean-Christophe, *au fait*, no doubt, with calming hysterical women, steers her out of the kitchen and into the courtyard where they can speak alone, observed only by television cameras trained on their every move.

'What can I do to help you?' asks Jean-Christophe.

'Just believe in me, just tell me I'm doing a good job –'

'How many times have I been telling you?'

Aby, her voice rising, interrupts. 'Can I speak? Let me speak. You tell me to listen – please listen to me.'

The chef is beginning to get the picture: Aby's problem is personal. It's all to do with him. 'Seriously, I have no intention to put somebody down,' he says. 'Therefore, there's something inside you which is obviously not working well between us.'

Aby, frustrated, flings a bottle of water at the wall. 'I hate the fact you never listen!' she shouts.

'Is that what you need to do?' says Jean-Christophe, taken aback by the outburst.

'I need to get it out,' she tells him. 'If I want to make a scene, I'll make a scene.'

Jean-Christophe does his best to calm her. He wants her to forget what has happened and return to work. She has just one request.

'I'm asking for an inch. Please, just an inch,' she says.

In the red kitchen, as service approaches, Gary Rhodes is in excellent spirits. Something in his bones tells him they're in for a good night, or perhaps he's just got wind that his rival is having staff problems.

'I'm in a winning mood, team,' he says. 'Tonight is our night. I feel positive. I feel like I've had a really good response from all of you today. We are going to stay on top.' Cheers go up in the red kitchen.

Among the celebrity diners are Paul Burrell and Liam Gallagher. Stein, in the blue kitchen, is beside himself at the sight of the Oasis singer.

As the food starts to arrive at the red kitchen pass, Gary is finally getting what he has been demanding from his team for days. He calls Sam over. 'Do you know what that is?' he asks, pointing at the steak she has just cooked.

'Medium rare,' she says.

'No. It's called perfection,' he says.

It's the starters coming through from Aaron, though, that produce the biggest compliment of the night. 'The scallops are to die for,' he tells him, planting a kiss on the cheek of the surprised trainee.

In the blue kitchen the chefs are doing their best to repeat their success of the night before, but the checks are coming in too fast and they're struggling to keep up. To Stein's delight, Liam Gallagher has ordered from the blue menu. What the trainee doesn't know is

that the singer has a bottle of ketchup and brown sauce on the table in case the food – most of which he ends up leaving anyway – fails to please.

When his meal – a complicated and colourful dish – arrives, the singer doesn't want it. He tips the food off the plate, saying, 'I haven't got the energy to eat it. If you put that in your body, man, you'd end up on the toilet all night.'

Fortunately, all this happens before Jean-Christophe goes to the table to thank him for choosing his menu.

When the chef returns to the kitchen with the singer in tow, Stein is overjoyed. 'It's surreal, like all my Christmases come at once,' he says, as Liam Gallagher scribbles an autograph on the trainee's T-shirt.

When the diners' verdicts come in, the red team is confident. They know they have done well, although in terms of covers the blue kitchen has done better – 54 blues compared with 28 reds. They have excelled with their cooking, however, scoring eight out of ten, compared with the blue kitchen's score of six.

'Your performance was outstanding,' Gary tells his team.

Elated, the reds head upstairs. For two members of the team – Aaron and Sam – it's not just their superlative cooking that has given them a warm feeling inside. They appear to be falling for each other, and they're not making any effort to be discreet.

'Aaron is really lovely,' says Sam. 'He's made it quite clear that he likes me and everything, which is really nice.'

In the red-team bedroom, Sam, perched on the edge of her bed, whispers, 'Are you going to take a shower?'

Aaron strips off his top. 'Yeah, let's get a shower.'

They disappear into the bathroom together. Quite what goes on no one knows since, due to an oversight, there are no cameras in there. No pictures, then, but a soundtrack will emerge in due course, courtesy of Stein.

MAIN COURSES

GARY RHODES

Roast Bitter Duck with Parsnip and Date Puree

SERVES 4

4 duck breasts, about 150 g each, skin on

3 to 4 tablespoons black treacle

2 fresh duck carcasses

125 g finely chopped vegetables (onions, carrots and celery)

70 ml Madeira

300 ml chicken stock (see Basics, page 94)

250 ml veal stock, boiled until reduced to a glossy glaze (see Basics, page 94)

FOR THE PARSNIP AND DATE PUREE:

500g parsnips

Half a small onion

1 clove

1 bay leaf

Some milk to cover

250g Medjool dates, stoned and chopped

Sea salt and freshly ground black pepper

Make the duck gravy. Chop the duck carcasses into even-sized pieces and roast in a hot oven until golden brown and the fat has rendered down. Drain bones in a colander to remove excess fat, saving some of the fat.

In a heavy-bottomed saucepan, sweat the onion, carrot and celery off in a little of the saved duck fat until golden brown.

Add the duck bones, deglaze with the Madeira, then cover with the chicken stock and veal glace and bring to the boil. Simmer sauce gently for 40 minutes, skimming regularly. Strain through a fine sieve and set aside.

For the purée, peel and core the parsnips, then cut into 5cm pieces and place in a heavy-bottomed saucepan. Cover with milk and add the onion. Bring to the boil and simmer until the parsnips are just tender. Drain in a colander, saving the milk and discarding the onion.

Place a little of the cooking milk in the bottom of a liquidiser and slowly add the cooked pieces of parsnips until a smooth purée has been formed. Rub through a sieve for a smooth texture. Season to taste. Set aside.

Put the chopped dates into a heavy-bottomed pan, cover with water, bring to the boil and simmer for 2 minutes, then drain the dates in a colander.

7 While still hot, liquidise the dates in a blender and add a little of the milk from the parsnip recipe. Rub through a sieve and season to taste.

8 Now mix together the parsnip and date purées, adding more parsnip purée in proportion, tasting as you go so the combined purée isn't too sweet. You may not need all the date purée.

9 Cook the duck breasts when ready to serve. Preheat the grill and heat a large frying pan until hot. Season the breasts and place skin side down in the pan. Fry over a moderate heat, allowing the skin to release excess fat while turning to a deep golden brown. Flip over and briefly cook the underside. Then turn back on the skin side, transfer to an ovenproof tray and brush with treacle. Place the tray under the grill until the treacle begins to sizzle, then rebrush each breast with the treacle and heat briefly again.

10 Reheat the purée and sauce. Spoon onto large warmed plates. Cut the breasts into 3 to 4 slices and arrange on the purée. Spoon over sauce or serve separately. Can be served with confit potatoes (see below) or baby new potatoes.

CONFIT POTATOES

SERVES 4
About 12 medium–small-sized potatoes
About 250 g salted butter, melted
Olive oil
Sea- salt flakes

1 Peel the potatoes, then cut into neat turned shapes, if liked. Preheat the oven to 150°C/Gas 2. Place the potatoes in a heavy-based roasting tray and pour over the butter.

2 Heat on top of the stove, just below simmering point. Then cover with a cartouche (a large sheet of greaseproof paper that just fits to the top of the tray) and cook in the oven until tender (about 45 minutes), turning once in the butter.

3 Before serving, the potatoes can be drained then fried over a moderate heat in olive oil until well coloured. Drain well and sprinkle with a few flakes of sea salt.

Baked Turbot with Spinach and a Mussel Risotto

SERVES 4

4 fillets of turbot, about 175 g each, skinned

A little flour for dusting, optional

Olive oil, for frying

A large knob of butter

150 g picked and washed spinach

Some acid butter, for drizzling

(see Basics, page 101)

Sea salt and freshly ground white pepper

FOR THE MUSSEL RISOTTO:

60 g unsalted butter plus extra knobs
to serve

1 kg fresh mussels, cleaned and bearded

2 onions, finely chopped

1 small glass white wine

1.3 litres fish stock (see Basics, page 95)

A squeeze of lemon juice

200 g Arborio risotto rice

40 g butter

1 onion, finely chopped

Chopped fresh mixed herbs to serve –

parsley, chives, chervil

1 First, cook the mussels. In a large saucepan, melt a third of the butter and gently cook half the chopped onion. Then pour in the white wine, 300 ml of fish stock and the lemon juice. Once boiling, add the mussels. (It's important the saucepan is only half-full of mussels for even cooking.)

2 Cover and cook on a high heat, shaking and stirring from time to time, until all mussels have opened. Drain in a colander, saving all of the cooking liquor, before passing it through a fine sieve or muslin cloth.

3 Separate the mussels from their shells, checking all have been previously bearded and do not hold any shell splinters. Set mussels and liquor aside.

4 For the risotto, melt the remaining butter in a large heavy-bottomed pan. Add the remaining chopped onion and cook gently without browning until softened. Stir in the rice and cook for several minutes, ensuring that all of the rice grains are evenly coated in butter.

5 Slowly add the litre of hot stock, a ladleful or two at a time, stirring it in well to the rice and making sure the stock is absorbed before you add more. Continue this method until the risotto is just two-thirds cooked (approximately 12 to 13 minutes), before removing from the heat and leaving to cool.

6 At this stage, prepare and cook the fish. Lightly dust the top side of each fillet with a touch of flour, if using. Season and pan-fry the turbot in a few drops of olive oil until a light golden brown. Turn the fish in the pan and cook for a few more minutes until just tender. Keep warm.

7 Blanch the spinach in a little boiling water, then drain well and mix with some acid butter.

8 Reheat, warm and loosen the part-cooked risotto, continuing the cooking process with the warmed mussel stock. Once tender, but left with a slight bite, fresh mussels and herbs can be stirred in, along with an extra knob or two of butter to enrich the finished flavour.

9 Present the turbot on a bed of spinach, drizzling with a little more acid butter. Offer the mussel risotto separately in a warm copper pan.

Fillet of Steak with Oxtail Cottage Pie and Gravy

SERVES 4

175 g to 200 g beef fillet

150 g baby leaf spinach

A good knob of butter

Sea salt and freshly ground black pepper

FOR THE OXTAIL PIE:

1 oxtail, trimmed of fat and cut in joints

A little beef dripping or olive oil

1 carrot, diced

1 small onion, chopped

1 celery stick, chopped

1 leek, chopped

100 g tomatoes, chopped

1 sprig of fresh thyme

1 bay leaf

1 garlic clove, crushed

200 ml red wine

600 ml veal stock (see Basics, page 94)

4 shortcrust pastry cases, cooked, about 10 cm diameter

200 g of finely diced carrot, swedes and turnips

Some creamy mashed potato (see Basics, page 97)

1 Cook the oxtail first. Season and fry in a large pan in the dripping or oil until brown on all sides, then drain in a colander.

2 Gently fry the carrot, onion, celery and leek in the same pan, collecting all the residue from the tails. Add the chopped tomatoes, thyme, bay leaf and garlic and continue to cook for a few minutes. Pour the red wine on top and boil to reduce by half. Place the oxtail in a braising pan on top of the stove with the vegetables, wine and stock.

3 Bring to a simmer, cover and braise gently for 2 to 2 ½ hours until the meat is tender and falling off the bone. Lift the pieces of meat from the sauce and keep to one side.

4 Rub the sauce through a fine sieve into a pan, then boil to reduce, skimming off all impurities, to a good sauce consistency. Repass through the sieve. Make sure the sauce is tasted at regular intervals while reducing.

5 Tear the meat into thick strands, removing all traces of gristle or fat. Boil the 200 g of diced root vegetables until just tender and mix with the meat and a little of the sauce. Check for seasoning.

6 Blanch the spinach in boiling salted water, drain, pressing to squeeze out excess water, then return to the pan and toss with some butter. To put the pies together, spoon the hot oxtail and vegetables into the pastry cases until flush with the border. Spoon or pipe the mashed potatoes on top through a plain 1 cm tube in a coned peak fashion. Keep the pies warm while you cook the steak.

7 Heat a heavy-based pan. Brush each steak with a little oil, season and pan-fry for about 3 minutes per side according to preference. Do not overcook beef fillet.

8 To complete the dish, present each beef fillet on a bed of cooked spinach with the oxtail cottage pie sitting beside. Serve the extra oxtail sauce separately.

Pan-fried Wild Salmon with English Asparagus and a Light Herb Casserole of peas and Broad Beans

SERVES 4

About 20 to 30 spears of asparagus

4 fillets of wild salmon, skin on

A little flour, for dusting

Some olive oil, for cooking

A good knob of butter, plus 50 g extra, melted for brushing

Coarse sea salt and freshly ground white pepper

FOR THE HERB CASSEROLE:

450 ml fish stock (ideally made with salmon bones) (see Basics, page 95)

120 g cooked peas

120 g cooked broad beans

Cold diced butter

3 spring onions, cut into round slices

Some chopped parsley, chervil and sorrel

1 Trim the spiky ears from along the asparagus stalks with the blade of a knife and break or cut the grey-white stalk base away, keeping the spears in uniform length.

2 Using tweezers or your fingernails, pull out any pin bones from the salmon fillets you can feel with your fingertips. Season the salmon fillet and lightly flour the skin sides only. Put a large pan of salted water on to boil for the asparagus.

3 Heat the cooking oil in a large frying pan and fry the fillets, skin side down, on a medium to hot heat for 6 to 7 minutes, not shaking or moving the dish, just allowing the skins to fry and crisp. Turn the fillets, add the knob of butter and remove the pan from the heat. The fish will continue to cook in the remaining residual heat.

4 For the casserole, boil the salmon stock until reduced by half. Add the peas, broad beans and spring onions. Reheat, then add the knobs of cold butter, shaking them in well to emulsify. Finish with the chopped herbs, seasoning with salt and pepper. The herb casserole is now ready to serve, presenting it in a warm copper pan. (A splash of double cream or crème fraîche can be added for a creamier finish, along with a squeeze of lemon or lime juice to sharpen the flavour.)

5 After cooking the fish, plunge the asparagus tips into the large saucepan of rapidly boiling salted water. Cook for just 2 to 3 minutes, until tender.

6 Lift the spears from the pan, drain well and brush with butter to add more flavour and create a shine.

7 Place the spears side by side on a plate and season with a sprinkle of coarse sea salt. Sit the crispy salmon on top, offering the casserole apart. This dish eats very well with Jersey Royal potatoes.

Buttered Potato with Soft Cream Cheese on Chervil and Creme Fraiche Leeks

SERVES 4

4 large baking potatoes,
e.g. Maris Piper or Desiree
About 250 g clarified butter –
enough to cover
4 medium-sized leeks, thinly sliced
and blanched
3 to 4 tablespoons crème fraîche
2 teaspoons chopped fresh chervil
A little acid butter, optional
(see Basics, page 101)
Some olive oil, optional

FOR THE CREAM CHEESE FILLING:

1 large shallot, sliced
1 tablespoon olive oil
50 g cream cheese (softened)
1 egg plus 1 egg yolk
2 tablespoons double cream
100 g Maroilles cheese or Wigmore, diced
Sea salt and ground black pepper

1 Preheat the oven to 180°C/Gas 4. Peel and trim the potatoes into neat round shapes. These can now have their 'centres' cut away or scooped out, leaving a 5 to 10 mm surrounding border and base. This is best achieved using a small knife firstly to mark and cut the surrounding border before cutting away to the base or simply scooping with a round Parisienne cutter. Place the peeled potatoes in cold water to prevent discoloration.

2 Heat the clarified butter until it starts to bubble, then pour into a deep heatproof dish and add the potatoes. Carefully place in the oven and cook for about 30 minutes until just tender. To make the filling, warm the olive oil in a frying pan, add the shallots and cook on a low heat until softened. Leave to cool.

3 Soften the cream cheese, and mix with the eggs, egg yolks and double cream. Add the sliced onions, seasoning and the diced cheese. Divide between the potatoes and place on a baking tray. When ready to serve, cook in the oven for 30 to 35 minutes.

4 Once cooked, it's best to leave the potatoes to rest for 5 to 6 minutes. This relaxes the filling, allowing it to set. If cooking a little in advance they can be rewarmed for 10 to 12 minutes in the oven just before serving. For a richer golden-brown finish, the fondants can be coloured under a preheated grill.

5 For the leeks, blanch in some boiling salted water then drain and mix with the crème fraîche, chervil and seasoning. Spoon the leeks into warmed shallow bowls, arranging the fondant potato on top. Finish with a few drops of beurre blanc and olive oil around if liked.

JEAN-CHRISTOPHE NOVELLI

Pan-fried Dover Sole with Piperade-style Vegetables

SERVES 4

2 whole Dover soles, about 800g to 1kg each
4 x 1 cm slices aubergine
1 yellow pepper, cored and cut in quarters
1 red pepper, cored and quartered
2 medium courgettes, halved and sliced
A little infused cumin oil (see Basics, page 102)
4 sticks lemon grass, slightly bruised
2 bay leaves
120 g aubergine caviar (see Basics, page 101)
12 asparagus spears, trimmed and blanched
Olive oil, for cooking
Seasoning

1 Fillet the soles, then skin. Set aside. You should have 8 neat fillets.
2 Pan-fry the aubergines in a little oil and season. Remove and fry the courgettes in a little more oil until tender. Remove.
3 Heat the oven to 190°C/Gas 5. Wrap the peppers in greaseproof paper en papillote and roast for about 20 minutes, then remove and cool. Return the courgettes to the pan with a little cumin oil, the lemon grass sticks and bay leaves. Reheat and keep warm. Remove the lemon grass sticks for using as a garnish and pat dry.
4 When ready to serve, heat a frying pan with a little oil and cook the soles on one side until golden brown and crisping slightly at the edges. Season in the pan, then turn carefully and cook the other side.
5 To serve, spoon a quarter of the aubergine caviar in the centre of 4 warmed plates. Top each with a red pepper half, then spoon in another quarter of aubergine caviar. Place an aubergine slice on top of the purée, then a hot sole fillet on that.
6 Repeat the layers again and skewer together with the lemon grass sticks.
7 Spoon the courgettes and pan juices around and serve with asparagus spears. Garnish with the tomato skins and aubergine crisps, see page 74.

DRIED TOMATO SKINS

Blanch 4 tomatoes and remove the skins. Place these on a metal tray with nonstick baking parchment. Heat the oven to 140°C/Gas 1. Season the skins and sprinkle lightly with olive oil. Heat for about 10 minutes in the oven until crisp. Remove and cool.

AUBERGINE CRISPS

Thinly slice half a small aubergine. Lay the slices on nonstick baking parchment, season and dry in the oven at 140°C/Gas 1 for about 20 minutes until crisp. Remove and cool.

Braised Fillet of Turbot with Curried Dauphinoise, Mussel Bouillon and Curry Velouté

SERVES 4

NOTE: START THE MUSSELS THE DAY BEFORE

Curried dauphinoise potatoes, (see page 76)

Cooked mussels, (see right)

Curried velouté, (see page 76)

4 fillets turbot, about 150 g each

Basil-infused olive oil, (see page 39)

Truffle olive oil

100 g caul fat, soaked in cold water *

Olive oil, for frying

Sprigs of fresh thyme and two cloves of garlic, lightly crushed

4 small knobs of unsalted butter

* Ask your butcher for caul fat/crepinette – it is a lacy membrane used to wrap up home-made sausages, etc.

1 Prepare the mussels the day before; make the dauphinoise potatoes and the sauce. Set aside.

2 Neaten the turbot fillets if necessary and set aside in a bowl. Trickle over basil oil, truffle oil and seasoning and infuse for 10 minutes.

3 Remove the fish from the oil and wipe off the excess. Using a large metal cutter about the same size as the fillets, cut out 4 rounds of dauphinoise potatoes. Press a potato round on top of each fillet.

4 Spread out the caul fat and cut into four. Wrap each fish tian in the caul. Heat the oven to 190°C/Gas 5.

5 Bring a steamer to the boil, line the basket with some foil and steam the fish tians for about 12 minutes until just firm. Remove and allow to stand for 5 minutes.

6 Heat a frying pan with some olive oil, the thyme sprigs and garlic cloves. Sauté the fish tians all over until lightly brown and place on a tray. Dot with some butter and put into the oven for 4 minutes to reheat. Remove and stand for 2 minutes before serving.

7 To serve: serve the fish hot with the mussels alongside and the sauce to accompany. Garnish of a *brunoise* of chopped and blanched carrot and celeriac, wild asparagus or samphire and baby shimiji mushrooms. Top with mustard cress and bean-sprout cress.

MUSSELS

500 g fresh mussels
20 g porridge oats
1 shallot, chopped
1 wine glass of white wine

1 Clean the mussels if necessary in clean running water then leave in a bowl covered with cold water and sprinkle over the porridge oats. Leave for 12 hours, then drain and rinse again.

2 Heat a large pan on the hob and when it feels hot toss in the mussels with the shallot and wine. Bring to the boil, cover and cook for just a minute, then strain into bowl, reserving the liquid, and cover the mussels with clingfilm.

3 When all the mussels open, remove them from the shells and keep warm. Reserve the liquid.

CURRY VELOUTÉ

4 tablespoons olive oil

3 onions, chopped

Half a red pepper, cored and chopped

4 cloves garlic, chopped

Half a dessertspoon chopped ginger

3 tomatoes, chopped

2 medium mangoes, peeled and diced

2 teaspoons ground cumin

1 tablespoon coriander seeds

1 tablespoon paprika

1 teaspoon garam masala

A third of a cinnamon stick

5 or 6 cloves

5 or 6 cardamom pods

1 star anise

2 teaspoons fennel seeds

2 teaspoons cumin seeds

1 tablespoon curry powder

1 tablespoon turmeric

1 x 400ml can coconut milk

Mussel liquid from above recipe

1 Heat the oil in a large saucepan and gently fry the onions, pepper, garlic and ginger for about 10 minutes until softened but not coloured. Stir in the tomatoes, mango, all the spices and coconut milk and mussel broth.

2 Cover and simmer gently for about 1 hour. Then remove and blitz in a blender until smooth.

3 Pass through a fine *chinoise* (sieve), season to taste and set aside.

CURRIED DAUPHINOISE

500 g waxy potatoes

500 ml single cream

2 cloves garlic

1 teaspoon mild curry powder

200 g grated Emmenthal cheese

Seasoning

1 Peel and slice the potatoes wafer thin, on a mandoline or in a food processor.

2 Boil the cream and infuse with the garlic and curry powder for 10 minutes, then remove the garlic.

3 Arrange the potatoes, cheese and cream in a shallow baking tray, seasoning each layer. Press the potatoes well under the cream.

4 Heat the oven to 150°C/Gas 2 and bake for 1 ½ hours, pressing the potatoes down under the cream if they rise to the top. Remove and cool with another tray resting on top to firm, then chill until set.

Butcher's Plate, According to Jean-Christophe's Mood

Serve the trotters in slices with the oxtail and some soft celeriac mash.

STUFFED TROTTER

MAKES 8 TROTTERS

8 pigs' trotters, hind leg

FOR THE BRAISING LIQUOR:

1 x 75 cl   bottle port

1.5 litres red wine

500 ml veal stock (see Basics, page 94)

200 ml   chicken stock (see Basics, page 94)

1 head of garlic, halved

2 teaspoons honey

500 g shallots, peeled and sliced

FOR THE STUFFING:

300g black pudding

A little olive oil, for frying

100 g chopped duck or chicken livers

2 braised lamb shanks,

125 g foie gras, sliced

200 g chicken mousse (see Basics, page 98)

10 medium bay leaves

1 Using a sharp razor, shave the trotters to remove the small hairs. Then with a very sharp boning knife, slice down the length of the trotter and start to remove the skin in small shaving motions. Cut around the bone but ensure you don't cut through the skin, as this affects the presentation later.

2 Gently pull the skin back until you reach the forefingers, then cut through the end of the knuckles. Pull the skin further back until you reach the hoof and manoeuvre the knife around the toenails – at the tip of the toe you should be able to remove the nails easily.

3 When all the skin has been freed, use a blowtorch to gently singe any remaining hairs.

4 Meanwhile, put the port, wine, two stocks, garlic head and honey into a large pan. Bring to the boil, then cook until reduced by a third. Then add the shallots and leave to infuse for 20 minutes.

5 Put the trotter skins into a roasting pan, and strain over the stock. Heat the oven to 150°C/Gas2. Cover and cook for about 1 ½ hours, checking after 45 minutes that the trotters are still submerged in the stock. When tender, remove from the oven. Strain the stock back into a pan and boil down until reduced to thick and glossy.

6 Return the trotter skins to the roasting pan and spoon over the reduced stock. Return to the oven and continue cooking, basting occasionally, until they are dark and glossy. Remove and cool.

7 Now make the stuffing. Slice the black pudding and pan-fry in a little oil until browned. Remove and lightly fry the foie gras until just lightly coloured. Remove and break into pieces.

8 Place the livers in a bowl. Pick the meat from the cooked lamb shanks and pull into large shreds. Add to the gizzards with the black pudding and foie gras then bind with the chicken mousse and add seasoning.

9 Lay out the trotters on a board and divide the stuffing inside them. Top each with a bay leaf and roll up tightly in lightly buttered foil. Roll each into a neat boudin sausage shape.

10 Place the rolls in a steamer and steam for 15 minutes until firm. Remove from the heat and rest for 5 minutes. Then peel off the foil to reveal the stuffed trotter. Slice to serve.

OXTAIL FAGGOTS

1 whole oxtail, about 1 kg weight
Seasoning and caster sugar, to season
400 g finely chopped vegetables (onions, carrots and celery)
500 ml red wine
A little plain flour, for dusting
About 1 litre veal stock (see Basics, page 94)
120 g foie gras
Some caul fat/crepinette
120 g black pudding, cut into small rounds
8 quails' eggs

1 Season the oxtail with salt and sugar. Leave for 4 hours then marinade for 12 hours in the wine and vegetables.

2 Remove the oxtail, pat dry then toss in flour. Heat some oil in a large frying pan and brown the oxtail. Remove to a roasting pan.

3 Strain off the red wine and boil until reduced down. Pan-fry the vegetables, then add the stock. Bring to the boil, then pour over the oxtail and cover. Bake in a low oven at 140°C/Gas 1 for about 4 hours until tender. Remove from the oven, then shred the meat from the oxtail and cool. Strain off the liquor into a pan.

4 Make marble-sized balls of foie gras. Cut off a sheet of clingfilm, and shape an eighth of the oxtail into a circle. Place a foie gras ball in the centre and draw up the clingfilm into a ball, twisting to seal. Repeat with the remaining oxtail meat and foie gras. Chill until set, then uncover, top each ball with a piece of black pudding and wrap each in caul fat/crepinette to small faggots.

5 Heat the pan of cooking liquor, add the faggots and cook, turning once or twice until set (about 6 minutes). Remove and cool.

6 Fry the eggs in a little hot oil, then remove and drain.

CELERIAC SOFT MASH

SERVES 8

1 large celeriac, about 750 g
A little fresh lemon juice
50 g butter
100 ml double cream

1 Peel and dice the celeriac, immediately dropping the pieces into a bowl
of cold water with lemon juice.
2 Boil the celeriac in plenty of salted water, for about 15 minutes, or until tender.
3 Drain and return the celeriac to the pan and heat on the hob to dry out
a little. Then either press the celeriac through a potato ricer into a big
bowl, or rub through a drum sieve, or simply use a potato masher.
4 Boil the butter and cream together and slowly beat into the creamy
celeriac. Season to taste and keep warm until ready to serve.

'I had the trotter and it was very good,
quite rich. I didn't finish it, but I'm on a diet.'
Antony Worrall Thompson

Tournedos of Scottish Beef Fillet with Portobello Mushroom and Beaufort Cheese Glacé

SERVES 4

4 beef fillet steaks, about 150 g each
4 large Portobello mushrooms
A little olive oil, for cooking
120 g tomato fondue (see Basics, page 102)
80 g Beaufort or Gruyere cheese, grated
4 medium-sized bay leaves

Seasoning
TO SERVE:
Pomme Carlos, see below
Red-wine sauce made with Barolo wine,
(see Basics, page 96)
Garnishes, see end of recipe

1 Trim the fillets of any sinew, then roll each tightly in clingfilm into a neat shape. Chill overnight.

2 Next day, make the Pomme Carlos, Barolo red-wine sauce and prepare garnishes.

3 When ready to serve, unwrap the steaks. Heat the oven to 200°C/Gas 6.

4 Using a metal cutter, cut the Portobello mushrooms into the same diameter as the beef fillet. Heat some oil in a frying pan and cook them until golden brown. Place on a metal baking tray.

5 Reheat the pan, adding extra oil if necessary. Unwrap the steaks, season and brown in the hot pan to seal. Remove and place each steak on a mushroom . Bake in the oven for about 4 minutes (for medium rare) or according to preference. Remove and set aside.

6 Preheat a grill. Spoon tomato fondue on top of each steak, sprinkle with the cheese. Make an incision in each steak and insert a bay leaf, then grill until hot and gratinéed.

6 Serve with Pomme Carlos and a garnish of sautéed button onions, sautéed Oriental hon-shimeji mushrooms, wilted baby leaf spinach and hot Barolo wine sauce.

POMME CARLOS

125 g unsalted butter
4 waxy potatoes, peeled

1 Melt the butter, then carefully pour off the golden oil. Discard the milky deposits.

2 Using a small paring knife, lightly trim each potato into a neat round then slice thinly, ideally on a Japanese-style mandoline.

3 Line a flat baking sheet with nonstick baking parchment and brush with half the butter. Then arrange the potato slices into four flower shapes. Brush the top of the potato with the remaining butter and cover with another sheet of nonstick baking paper.

4 Preheat the oven to 200°C/Gas 6. Place a small metal tray flat on top of the paper-lined potatoes and cook for about 25 minutes until golden brown, checking halfway through. Uncover, peel off the top paper and slide the cooked potato 'flowers' onto a wire tray to cool.

Cutlet of Welsh Lamb with Beenleigh Blue Cheese Souffle, Braised Lentils and Lamb Jus

SERVES 4

8 Welsh lamb cutlets
200 g chicken mousse (see Basics, page 98)
80 g Beenleigh blue cheese
100 g caul fat/crepinette
8 large basil leaves, blanched and patted dry
10 g each thyme and rosemary sprigs

FOR THE SAUCE:

1k g fresh lamb bones
250 g finely chopped vegetables
(onions, carrots and celery)
300 ml dry white wine
1 litre veal stock (see Basics, page 94)
Lamb fat, from the trimmings

FOR THE LENTILS:

100 g cooked Puy or green lentils
1 shallot, chopped
20 g each diced carrots, leeks, celery
2 fresh cloves garlic
A knob of butter
Some fresh chopped parsley

FOR THE GARNISH:

400 g mashed potato (see Basics, page 97)
16 baby onions, peeled
16 roasted garlic cloves
4 large aubergine crisps (see page 74)

1 Trim the lamb cutlets so there is no fat or skin. Reserve the fat for the sauce.

2 Beat out each cutlet with a rolling pin to flatten. Then season and lay out on a board.

3 Spread with the chicken mousse. Top with the cheese and the basil leaves. Wrap in the caul fat/crepinette. Set aside in the fridge while you make the sauce.

4 Brown the lamb bones in a hot oven, then place in a large saucepan with the onion, carrot and celery, the wine, stock and seasoning. Bring to the boil, simmer until reduced by half, then strain and set aside.

5 To cook the lentils, place in a pan and cover with cold water. Bring to the boil, then drain and rinse in cold water.

6 Heat some oil in the same pan and sauté the shallots, diced vegetables and garlic cloves for about a minute. Add the blanched lentils, then the lamb stock. Simmer until tender (about 15 minutes). Stir in a knob of butter and chopped parsley.

7 Pan-fry the wrapped lamb cutlets in a little hot oil until golden brown on both sides (about 3 minutes each side), adding the thyme and rosemary sprigs at the end of cooking.

8 To serve, spoon the potato in the centre of 4 warmed plates, spoon around the roasted garlic and sit 2 cutlets each on top. Surround with the baby onions and roasted garlic. Top with the aubergine crisp. Spoon the lentil sauce around and serve.

Daube De Boeuf with Sauce Aigre Doux

SERVES 6

1.5 kg unsalted beef – silverside or
top rump joint
125 g piece pork fat – in one piece
3 large carrots, sliced
1 large onion, sliced thinly
2 sticks celery, sliced
Half a bottle red wine
4 tablespoons red wine vinegar
A few handfuls parsley stalks,
thyme sprigs and 2 tarragon sprigs
2 bay leaves
Half a teaspoon black peppercorns

2 star anise
A little olive oil
300 ml veal stock (see Basics, page 94)
100 g raisins, soaked
1 tablespoon brandy
142 ml pot double cream

FOR THE GARNISH:

Baby carrots and turnips, trimmed
Fresh peas and asparagus tips
A little butter
Sea salt and freshly ground black pepper

1 Untie the joint if it is trussed. Cut the fat into long thin strips, thread them onto a larding needle, then draw them evenly through the meat. Place the larded joint into a deep dish with the vegetables, wine, vinegar, herbs, peppercorns and star anise.

2 Cover the dish and leave for at least 24 hours, turning the joint in the marinade 2 or 3 times. Remove the meat and pat dry, then heat a heavy frying pan until hot. Brush the beef with some oil and brown it in the hot pan, turning until a nice brown colour. Season well in the pan.

3 Strain the liquid from the vegetables and reserve. Place the meat in a deep ovenproof dish and pack the marinade vegetables around it along with the herbs and star anise. Discard the peppercorns. Heat the oven to 170°C/Gas 3.

4 Cover the dish tightly and bake the beef for about 2 ½ to 3 hours or until it is very tender when pierced. Remove from the oven and allow to stand, still covered, for 15 minutes, then strain the cooking juices into a saucepan along with the marinade liquid.

5 Boil down the liquid until reduced by half, then add the stock, soaked raisins and brandy. Boil again until reduced by half and stir in the cream. Boil for another 5 minutes, then taste for seasoning.

6 Blanch the garnish vegetables and toss with some butter. Remove the beef (discarding the cooking vegetables), slice and serve with the dressed vegetables and sauce

Vegetarian Red Onion, Broccoli and Roquefort Strudel

SERVES 4

2 red onions, sliced thinly

100 ml olive oil

1 teaspoon fresh thyme leaves

2 tablespoons balsamic vinegar

250 g shitake mushrooms, sliced

250 g broccoli florets, long stalks trimmed off

1 pack filo pastry, thawed if frozen

75 g butter, melted

200 g Roquefort cheese, crumbled

Wild rocket, baby leaf spinach and chicory leaves, to serve

Vinaigrette dressing (see Basics, page 99)

Sea salt and freshly ground black pepper

1 Sauté the sliced onions in half the oil for about 10 minutes until softened. Season, add the thyme and vinegar and cook for 2 more minutes. Remove to a bowl. Add more oil and the mushrooms and stir-fry over a high heat until browned and lightly softened. Season and remove to the onions.

2 Blanch the broccoli florets in boiling salted water for 5 minutes, then drain well and run under a cold tap for a minute or so until cool. Drain well again and cut any large florets into smaller pieces. Pat dry with paper towel.

3 Cover a large flat metal baking tray with nonstick baking paper and cover with single sheets of filo to about 50 x 25 cm. Brush lightly with some of the melted butter and top with more filo. Repeat like this until you have 4 layers of filo. You may not need the whole pack of filo.

4 Scatter over the onions and mushrooms, then sprinkle over the broccoli and finally break over little chunks of Roquefort. Season well with pepper. Roll up from the long edge using the edge of the paper to lift up the pastry so it rolls evenly.

5 When you have a long roll, brush the top with any remaining butter. Pinch the ends together so the filling stays inside.

6 Chill these while you preheat the oven to 190°C/Gas 5. Bake for about 20 to 25 minutes until golden and crisp, then set aside to cool for 10 to 15 minutes.

7 Make a salad with the rocket, spinach and chicory leaves. Toss with the dressing and season.

8 Cut the strudel into 4 to 8 diagonal slices and place on a plate with the salad alongside.

Monkfish in Pancetta with Provençale Vegetables and Sauce Vierge

SERVES 4

1 monkfish tail, about 800 g to 900 g

Leaves from 1 sprig fresh thyme

100 g pancetta, sliced very thinly

2 peppers, red or yellow, cored and quartered

1 large courgette, cut in neat sticks

Half a small aubergine, cut in small neat chunks

6 medium–small plum tomatoes, peeled and halved

Extra-virgin olive oil, to drizzle

Flat-leaf parsley leaves, to serve

FOR THE SAUCE:

Half a teaspoon crushed coriander berries

1 small shallot, finely chopped

1 clove garlic, crushed

6 large leaves fresh basil, shredded

Leaves from 2 large sprigs fresh tarragon, chopped

2 tablespoons fresh lemon juice

2 teaspoons balsamic vinegar

100 ml extra-virgin olive oil

1 Trim all the grey membrane from the monkfish tail using a very sharp filleting knife. Then remove both fillets from the central bone. Season, sprinkle with thyme and place back together in opposite directions, i.e. nose to tail, so you have a fillet of equal thickness.

2 Spread out the pancetta slices on a sheet of clingfilm in a rectangle large enough to wrap over the tail. Place the monkfish in the centre and wrap up tightly in the clingfilm, twisting the ends. Chill for a good 6 hours to set the shape.

3 Heat the oven to 180°C/Gas 4. Toss together the peppers, courgette and aubergine in some oil.

4 Heat a large nonstick pan and add a little oil, swirling to coat the pan base. Unwrap the monkfish and sauté for a few minutes, turning to brown it all over. Remove from the pan to a plate.

5 Add the oil-coated vegetables to the pan and cook, stirring once or twice on a medium heat until lightly browned. Add the tomatoes and seasoning. Cook a few minutes more until softened. Then transfer to a roasting dish and place the monkfish on top.

6 Roast in the oven for around 10 to 15 minutes depending on the thickness of the fish. You can test this by pressing with your finger. If it is just firm, it is done. Remove from the oven and stand.

7 Meanwhile, mix together all the sauce ingredients and simmer until reduced by half. Slice the monkfish into 8 and place on 4 warmed plates. Scatter the vegetables around and spoon over the sauce. Garnish with the parsley sprigs and serve.

Guinea Fowl with Tagliatelle and Cep Velouté

SERVES 4
1 quantity cep velouté (see Basics, page 96)
2 guinea fowl, about 1 kg each
1 litre chicken stock (see Basics, page 94)
25 g butter
300 g to 400 g fresh tagliatelle, or linguine
Sea salt and freshly ground black pepper
FOR THE GARNISH:
250 g broad beans
250 g asparagus tips
Knob of butter

1 Make the cep velouté in advance. Detach the legs and wings from the guinea fowl. (These can be used elsewhere, e.g. in a casserole.) This leaves you with just the breasts on the carcass.

2 Bring the stock to the boil in a large pan and submerge the carcasses breast side down into the pot so they are covered with stock. Return to a gentle simmer and cook for 8 minutes only. Remove the carcasses from the stock and cool for 10 minutes. The stock can be used again, elsewhere.

3 Using a sharp knife, remove the breasts from the carcass with the skin attached, in one piece. Heat the butter in a large sauté pan and brown the breasts skin side down for about 3 minutes, then flip over and cook the other side for another 3 minutes. Allow to stand.

4 Prepare the garnish. Blanch the broad beans and asparagus in boiling water for 2 minutes, then drain and plunge into iced water. Drain again and pop the beans from their skins. Return to a saucepan with a small knob of butter.

5 Boil the tagliatelle for about 3 minutes, then drain. Mix with a little of the velouté.

6 To serve, slice each breast in 3 or 4 on the diagonal. Divide the tagliatelle between 4 warmed plates. Sit the slices of breast on top.

7 Reheat the vegetables in the butter and spoon around, then drizzle over the remaining sauce and serve.

Braised Lamb Shanks with Parsnip Purée and Roasted Root Vegetables

SERVES 4

4 large lamb shanks

A little olive oil

1 onion, chopped

2 carrots, chopped, plus 2 extra to serve

1 leek, chopped

1 stick celery, chopped

Half a head of garlic

2 sprigs each fresh thyme and rosemary

2 bay leaves

1 litre brown chicken stock (see Basics, page 95)

Half a bottle red wine

Sea salt and freshly ground black pepper

VEGETABLES, TO SERVE:

500 g parsnips, peeled and chopped

A good knob of butter

2 to 3 tablespoons double cream

250 g salsify

A squeeze of lemon juice

4 baby fennels, split in half

1 Heat the oven to 180°C/Gas 4. Fry the lamb shanks in a frying pan with a little oil until browned all over. Transfer to a roasting pan. Add the vegetables to the pan and brown also. Tip into the same roasting pan along with the herb sprigs and seasoning.

2 Meanwhile, prepare the vegetables for roasting. Peel the extra carrots and cut into neat sticks. Peel the salsify and rinse in cold water with a squeeze of lemon juice, then drain. Slit the fennels in half lengthwise. Toss these three vegetables together with some oil and shake out into an ovenproof dish. Season on top.

3 Boil the stock and wine together for about 3 minutes, then pour over the lamb shanks. Cover with foil and bake for about 40 minutes, then uncover and baste. Return to the oven and cook uncovered for a further 20 minutes until the meat is tender. Remove the shanks and keep warm.

4 At the same time, put the pan of roasting vegetables on the top shelf and cook for about 20 minutes until just tender, stirring once. Remove and set aside.

5 Strain off the lamb pan juices into a saucepan and boil until reduced to a rich sauce, about 300 ml. Set aside. Discard the lamb vegetables.

6 Meanwhile, peel and roughly chop the parsnips. Boil in salted water until tender. Drain and whiz to a purée in a food processor or blender, adding a knob of butter and the cream. Pass through a sieve and rub with the back of a ladle, season and set aside.

7 To serve, spoon the parsnip purée into the centre of 4 warmed dishes. Sit a shank on top and surround with the roasted vegetables. Reheat the sauce until boiling and pour around the plates. Serve hot.

Giant Open Ravioli with Salmon and Baby Leeks

SERVES 4

250 g 'oo' pasta flour or plain flour
Quarter of a teaspoon fine sea salt
2 free-range eggs
1 tablespoon olive oil
FOR THE FILLING:
400 g fillet fresh salmon, skinned
A little extra-virgin olive oil
250 g baby leeks, trimmed and halved
300 ml fish stock (see Basics, page 95)

200 g crème fraîche
2 tablespoons Noilly Prat or other
dry vermouth
2 teaspoons chopped fresh chervil
1 tablespoon chopped fresh chives
Sprigs of fresh chervil or long chives
to garnish
250 g baby-leaf spinach
Sea salt and freshly ground black pepper

1 First, make the pasta. Put the flour, salt, eggs and oil into a food processor and pulse until it starts to form coarse crumbs.

2 Tip this out onto a worktop and knead with your hands to a smooth dough, adding sprinkles of cold water if necessary. Wrap in clingfilm and leave to rest for 30 minutes.

3 Now make the filling. Preheat the grill. Brush the tops of the salmon fillets with some oil and season. Grill both sides for about 6 minutes in total until just firm but not dry. Remove, cool and break into chunks, pulling out any stray bones you may find.

4 Blanch the baby leeks also in salted water for about 3 minutes then drain well and pat dry. Stir-fry the spinach in some more hot oil, until wilted, and season. Drain and keep warm.

5 Boil together the stock, crème fraîche and vermouth until reduced by a third. Check the seasoning and mix in the herbs. Mix a little with the salmon to moisten.

6 Now roll out the pasta, use a pasta-rolling machine. Break off chunks of dough and feed through the rollers several times, starting with the thickest setting and gradually turning it down a notch every 2 to 3 rollings until you get to the final thin setting.

7 Cut out 12 rounds about 15 to 17 cm diameter. Drop the 4 rounds into a large pan of salted water and boil for about 2 minutes until softened. Drain. Divide the spinach between four warmed plates in the centre and place a pasta round on top. Spoon over half the salmon and leeks.

8 Boil the remaining pasta rounds in two batches, topping with another set of 4 rounds and spooning over the remaining salmon and leeks. Finally, top with the last rounds. Reheat the remaining sauce and spoon over each ravioli. Garnish with the herbs and serve.

MAIN COURSE
BASICS

Veal Stock

MAKES ABOUT 2 LITRES

1 kg veal bones, chopped

250 g chicken necks

1 calf's foot

Cold water, to cover

1 onion, chopped

4 carrots, chopped

2 large leek, chopped

3 sticks celery, chopped

250 ml tomato juice

1 tablespoon brandy

3 tablespoons white wine

1 Put the bones, necks and calf's foot into a large stockpot. Cover with at least 5 litres of cold water; bring to the boil, skimming occasionally any scum that rises, using a metal spoon.

2 Simmer gently for 4 hours then add the vegetables and continue simmering for 2 hours.

3 Pour through a large sieve lined with wet muslin. Add the tomato juice, brandy and wine, cool and chill until required. Freeze in portions about 500 ml each.

Chicken Stock

MAKES ABOUT 2 LITRES

2 kg chicken wings

Cold water

1 onion

2 leeks

2 sticks celery

2 sprigs fresh thyme

1 Cover the chicken wings with about 5 litres of water in a large stockpot. Bring to the boil and simmer gently for 2 hours. Add the vegetables and thyme. Simmer for a further 2 hours.

2 Strain through a muslin-lined sieve, cool and chill or freeze.

Brown Chicken Stock

MAKES ABOUT 2 LITRES

2 kg chicken wings
A little olive oil
500 g finely chopped vegetables (onions, carrots and celery)
1 head garlic, halved
2 or 3 sprigs fresh thyme

1 Sauté the chicken wings in a little oil in a large stock pan until caramelised. Add the vegetables, cover with about 3 litres of cold water, add the garlic and herbs and bring to boil.
2 Skim off any scum that rises and simmer for 2 hours.
3 Strain through a muslin-lined sieve. Cool, chill and freeze.

Fish Stock

MAKES ABOUT 1 LITRE

2 kg fresh bones, not heads, preferably sole or turbot
1 onion, chopped
2 leeks, chopped
1 stick celery, chopped
5 peppercorns
2 sprigs fresh thyme
2 bay leaves

1 Wash the bones under running water until clean.
2 Add everything to the pan and cover with about 2.5 litres of cold water. Bring to the boil and simmer for 20 minutes, then remove from the heat and leave to sit for 20 minutes.
3 Pass through a muslin-lined sieve and return to the pan. Boil until reduced to 1 litre, then chill until required. Use within 2 days or freeze.

Red Wine Sauce

MAKES 500 ML

2 shallots, sliced

2 tablespoons olive oil

Half a head of garlic

15 g butter

1 sprig fresh thyme

100ml red wine, e.g. Barolo

3 tablespoons port

1 litre veal stock

1 Sauté the shallots in the oil for about 10 minutes until caramelised. Add the garlic, butter and thyme, then the wine.

2 Boil until reduced right down. Pour in the port and veal stock and boil until reduced by half.

3 Strain through a muslin-lined sieve, cool and chill.

Cep Velouté

MAKES ABOUT 1 LITRE

1 kg chicken wings

3 tablespoons olive oil

5 shallots, sliced

1 head of garlic

1 x 75 cl bottle dry white wine

2 litres chicken stock

300 ml double cream

25 g dried cep (porcini) mushrooms

4 sprigs fresh thyme

1 Sauté the chicken wings in the oil in a large saucepan until golden brown.

2 Add the shallots and brown with the bones, then add the garlic and dried mushrooms.

3 Deglaze with the white wine boiling until reduced by half. Add the stock and the thyme and reduce again by half.

4 Stir in the cream and boil for about 10 minutes. Remove from the heat. Allow to stand for 15 minutes, then strain through a fine sieve. Cool and use as required. Can be frozen in smaller amounts.

Port Sauce

MAKES ABOUT 1 LITRE

5 shallots, sliced

Half a head of garlic

3 tablespoons olive oil

2 large carrots, chopped

500 g button mushrooms

300 ml port

2 litres veal or chicken stock

1 Sauté the shallots and garlic in the oil in a large saucepan for about 10 minutes until lightly browned. Add the carrots and cook for 5 minutes, then mix in the mushrooms, adding extra oil if necessary. Cook for 5 more minutes on a high heat.

2 Pour in the port and deglaze by three quarters. Finally add the stock and boil until reduced by half.

3 Cool for 10 minutes, then strain through a fine sieve. Chill or freeze in smaller amounts.

Mashed Potatoes

SERVES 6 TO 8

1 kg Maris Piper potatoes, peeled

50 g butter

125 ml double cream

Seasoning

1 Boil the potatoes in plenty of salted water to cover, for about 15 minutes, until tender.

2 Drain and return the potatoes to the pan and heat on the stove to dry out a little. Then either press the potatoes through a potato ricer into a big bowl, or rub through a drum sieve, or simply use a potato masher.

3 Boil the butter and cream together and slowly beat into the creamy potatoes. Season to taste and keep warm until ready to serve.

Chicken Mousse

USED FOR BINDING MIXTURES
MAKES ABOUT 500 G
250 g chicken breast, skinned and roughly chopped
Half a teaspoon sea salt
1 egg white
300 ml double cream

1 Chill the bowl of a food processor in the freezer for 10 minutes. Blitz the chicken breast for about 20 seconds, then return the bowl with the chicken mixture to the freezer and leave for 10 minutes. Repeat this 3 more times until the flesh is very smooth.
2 Then mix in the egg white and the cream. Give a final blitz, then rub the mixture through a fine sieve.

Red-wine Dressing

MAKES ABOUT 150 ML
2 teaspoons Dijon mustard
2 tablespoons red-wine vinegar (if using Cabernet Sauvignon, add 1 ½ teaspoons, adding more once finished, if preferred)
1 egg yolk or 1 tablespoon bought mayonnaise
4 tablespoons walnut oil
4 tablespoons groundnut oil
Sea salt and pepper

1 Using a balloon whisk, beat together the mustard, vinegar and egg yolk or mayonnaise in a bowl.
2 Mix together the two oils and slowly and gradually whisk them into the mustard and vinegar. The oil will emulsify with the base ingredients. Season with salt and pepper. Store in a screw-topped jar and chill until required.

Fragrant Vinaigrette Dressing

MAKES ABOUT 600 ML

300 ml extra-virgin olive oil

300 ml groundnut oil

3 tablespoons balsamic vinegar

A bunch of fresh basil

A small bunch of fresh tarragon

3 or 4 sprigs of thyme

12 black peppercorns, lightly crushed

3 shallots, finely chopped

1 bay leaf

1 teaspoon coarse sea salt

1 Warm the olive and groundnut oils together. Push all the remaining ingredients in a wide-necked bottle, at least 75 cl. Pour the oil into the bottle and close with a cork or screw top.

2 For the best results, leave to marinate for a week, which will allow all the flavours to enhance the oil. To help the dressing along, shake the bottle once a day. Taste for seasoning before using.

Vinaigrette

MAKES ABOUT 500 ML

250 ml groundnut oil

250 ml olive oil

3 tablespoons white-wine vinegar

Juice of 1 lemon

2 teaspoons sea salt

1 teaspoon freshly ground pepper

Blitz everything together in a blender or food processor. Store in a bottle in the fridge and use as required.

Sherry Vinegar Dressing

MAKES ABOUT 120 ML

FOR THE INFUSION:
2 tablespoons sherry vinegar
2 tablespoons light, soft brown sugar
75 g seedless white grapes
FOR THE DRESSING:
100ml single cream

3 tablespoons walnut oil
2 tablespoons infusion
Some chopped fresh chives
A dash of truffle oil
A squeeze of lemon juice
Sea salt and freshly ground black pepper

1 Blitz together the sherry vinegar, sugar and grapes to a purée. Then remove
2 tablespoons and whisk with the cream, walnut oil and some seasoning. Add
the chives and the lemon juice to taste and finally a dash of truffle oil.
2 The remaining grape infusion can be chilled for another batch of dressing.

Hollandaise Sauce

MAKES ABOUT 300 ML

250 g unsalted butter
2 teaspoons white-wine vinegar
1 teaspoon cracked white peppercorns

A pinch of salt
4 free-range egg yolks
A squeeze of lemon juice

1 Melt the butter in a saucepan over a low heat until it starts to foam. Spoon
off the foam and leave the butter to settle.
2 Remove the clarified butter with a ladle, discarding the milky residue remaining
in the pan. Keep the butter to one side.
3 Beat the vinegar and peppercorns with 2 tablespoons of water and the yolks
in a medium-sized bowl.
4 Then place this over a pan of gently simmering water and continue whisking to a
thick creamy foam (approximately 8 to 10 minutes). Do not let the mixture overheat.
5 Remove from the heat and, whisking continuously, slowly pour in the clarified butter
until you have a thick yellow sauce. Pass through a fine sieve and add a squeeze of
lemon juice to taste.

Acid Butter

MAKES ABOUT 350 G

150 ml white wine vinegar

300 ml white wine

1 onion, sliced thinly

250g butter, diced

1 Cook together the vinegar, wine and onions in a saucepan until reduced to a thick syrup mix.

2 Gradually beat in the butter until blended, then remove and cool. Scoop into a container and chill until required. Scoop out spoonfuls as required. Great with vegetables or added to sauces.

Aubergine Caviar

MAKES ABOUT 400 G

2 aubergines, sliced

200 ml olive oil

3 garlic cloves

2 sprigs fresh thyme

1 teaspoon sea salt

1 teaspoon caster sugar

1 Slice the aubergines and place in a deep pan. Add the remaining ingredients and heat to medium, then cook gently for about 30 minutes until tender.

2 Remove from the heat, and blitz until smooth. Cool, check the seasoning and use as required.

Tapenade

MAKES ABOUT 250 G

175 g black olives, stoned

40 g anchovies

100 ml olive oil

1 garlic clove

Blitz all the ingredients till smooth. Store in a screw-topped jar in the fridge and use as required.

Tomato Fondue

MAKES ABOUT 120 G

3 tomatoes

1 small shallot, finely chopped

1 small clove garlic, crushed

½ teaspoon of sugar

1 teaspoon white wine vinegar

1 Blanch the tomatoes in boiling water for a few seconds, then peel the skins, halve, de-seed and chop the flesh.

2 Cook together the shallot, garlic, sugar and vinegar with a little water until softened and reduced. Mix in the tomatoes and cook for a few minutes more until soft and pulpy.

Cep Oil

MAKES 200 ML

100 g fresh ceps or porcini

200 ml extra-virgin olive oil

2 sprigs fresh thyme

1 Pan-fry the ceps in a little of the oil until lightly browned and the scent is strong.

2 Add the thyme and remaining oil. Heat to 60°C then remove from the heat and stand until cool.

3 Infuse for 24 hours, then strain into a bottle and store in the fridge.

Flavoured Oils

250 ml extra-virgin olive oil

CHOOSE FROM:

20 to 30 g fresh basil sprigs

1 teaspoon cumin seeds

125 g chopped chorizo sausage

2 cloves garlic, crushed

2 sprigs fresh thyme and rosemary

Small bunch each tarragon and chives

1 Heat the oil until it reaches 60°C, then add one or more of the above flavourings plus seasoning.

2 Cool for 24 hours, then strain into a bottle. Keep chilled until required.

Dried Aubergine, Carrot or Tomato Slices

1 thin aubergine or 2 large carrots or 6 firm medium-sized tomatoes
A little softened butter
Fine sea salt

1 Top and tail the vegetable of your choice, then thinly slice at an angle, to produce oval-shaped slices about 2 mm thick. Cover a flat baking tray with a sheet of nonstick baking paper and lightly grease with the butter. Sprinkle evenly with a thin layer of salt (this helps to draw out the moisture from the vegetable).
2 Lay the aubergine or carrot slices on top in a single layer. Lightly grease another sheet of paper and press, butter side down, on top. Then place another metal baking sheet on top to keep the slices flat.
3 Heat the oven to its lowest setting and bake the two sheets for about 2 to 4 hours or until the vegetables are crisp and dried.
4 Peel off the paper sheets and remove to a wire rack to cool completely. Store in an airtight container.

Parmesan Crackling

MAKES ABOUT 12 WAFERS
100 g Parmesan cheese, finely grated
Coarsely ground black pepper, optional

1 Heat the oven to 160°C/Gas 3. Cover a flat baking tray with a sheet of nonstick baking paper.
2 Sprinkle teaspoonfuls of grated cheese onto the paper in neat 4 to 5 cm rounds, well spaced to allow for spreading. Scatter with black pepper, if liked, then bake until the cheese starts to melt and bubble and turn golden brown.
3 Meanwhile, upend metal tablespoons on a worktop. Scoop the melted parmesan gently off using a palette knife and lay on top of each spoon so it sets into an attractive shape. When cool and crisp, remove carefully and store in an airtight container until required.

SIGNATURE DISHES

ABY KING
Sexy Chicken

4 chicken breasts cut into goujon strips
75 ml bottle garlic-infused olive oil
½ carton Moroccan spice blend (I use La Karma blend from Fresh and Wild)
1 x 250 g pack Sammy's lemon-flavoured easy-cook couscous
50 g raisins
1 red pepper, cored and diced
1 yellow pepper, cored and diced
2 handfuls of fresh breadcrumbs (white or granary)
1 bunch of fresh mint, roughly torn
1 x 500 g carton Greek yogurt (medium-sized pot)
4 tablespoons orange-blossom honey

1 Marinate the chicken goujons in the spice blend and garlic olive oil, cover and chill for 15 minutes.
2 Measure out half a cup (125 ml) of couscous and place in a pan with 250ml boiling water. Return to the boil, then remove, cover and allow to stand for 4 minutes. Fork through well and mix in the peppers and raisins plus a few drizzles of the oil.
3 Put the breadcrumbs into a large mixing bowl. Mix in the mint, yogurt and honey. Remove the chicken goujons from the fridge and dunk into the breadcrumbs, shaking off any excess.
4 Heat the oil in a deep-sided frying pan and add the chicken in batches, frying until crisp and golden.
5 Reheat the couscous and serve with the crispy chicken.

'The whole thing feels like some really weird dream, it really does. I'm in the kitchen, haring around making marzipan trees and battling with a sex god.' Aby

AARON SIWOKU

Sea Bass with Pesto Mash

1 sea bass fillet (descaled), about 1.5 kg
50 g butter
Extra-virgin olive oil
450 g potatoes (Desiree or King Edward)
120 g fresh pesto
Sea salt
Freshly ground black pepper or whole peppercorns
Purple-sprouting broccoli

1 First begin to prepare the pesto mash. Use a potato peeler to remove the skins as
thinly as possible and then cut the potatoes into even-sized chunks, not too small.
If they are large, quarter them and if they are small, halve them. Put the potato chunks
in a large saucepan, then pour boiling water over them, add 1 dessertspoon of salt,
put on a lid and simmer gently until they are absolutely tender – they should take
approximately 25 minutes, so in the meantime there's time to sort out the fish (rub
it with sea salt, put some slits in the skin side so it doesn't curl up when being fried)
and get the purple-sprouting broccoli ready to steam.
2 When the potatoes are cooked, drain them; at the same time, start steaming the
broccoli. Cover them with a clean tea towel to absorb some of the steam for about
5 minutes, then add the pesto and a seasoning of salt and pepper. Using an electric
hand whisk, start whisking at a slow speed to break up the potatoes, then increase
the speed to fast and whip them up to a smooth purée.
3 Now it's time to fry the fish. Put some virgin olive oil in the pan, let it heat up
slightly, then place the fish skin side down into the pan. After 2 minutes turn it gently,
as it'll be slightly more delicate because of the slits we put in earlier. Give it another
2 minutes in the pan and ensure it's fully cooked by having a mooch into one of the
slits – it should be totally white with no light pinkie flesh whatsoever. Now return
the saucepan to a low heat and use a wooden spoon to turn the potatoes round until
they become hot – about 1 minute – and season. They're now ready to serve.
4 Place the pesto mash slightly off centre on the plate. Your purple-sprouting broccoli
should now be ready; check it with a knife, it should insert easily into the stems'
centre. Arrange the broccoli beside the mash, not allowing it to sit too flat as it will
prevent the plate from having a bit of dimension.
5 Finally, drizzle some fine extra-virgin olive oil across the fish to give it something
extra. Take it easy, though. It doesn't want to be swimming in it!

CAROLINE GARVEY
Pork Galliano and Herbs

1 pork tenderloin fillet, about 350 g
25 g of butter
2 tablespoons olive oil
1 tablespoon chopped fresh herbs; choose from
oregano, basil, tarragon, thyme and parsley
3 tablespoons Galliano
Sprigs of fresh herbs
1 fresh fig, sliced
Sea salt and ground black pepper

1 Trim fillet and slice diagonally into 2 cm pieces. Bash gently with a mallet
or rolling pin to flatten a little, then season.
2 Heat half the butter and oil in a frying pan until it starts to sizzle and brown.
3 Quickly toss in half the chopped herbs, then half the slices of pork, and brown
nicely, being careful not to overcrowd the pan. Set aside in a warmed dish and
repeat with the remaining herbs and pork.
4 Return the first batch of meat to the pan and pour over the Galliano. Flambé
with a match and quickly turn the meat in the pan juices, adding a little water
to moisten.
5 Season again and transfer into a serving dish. Garnish with the herb sprigs
and sliced fig.

'The chef's a perfectionist and if that
means he's got to have a go at me or not
have a go at me, or whatever, that's fine
really.' Caroline

GARY TOMLIN
Jerk Chicken

4 chicken-leg quarters (thigh and drumstick)

FOR THE JERK SEASONING

1 tablespoon garlic powder

1 tablespoon paprika

1 bunch fresh thyme

1 tablespoon pimento powder

2 teapoons sea salt

1 tablespoon coarse black pepper

2 tablespoons bottled jerk seasoning

50 ml white wine vinegar

4 cloves fresh garlic, crushed

1 Scotch bonnet chilli pepper, chopped finely

FOR THE COLESLAW

1 carrot, grated coarsely

1 onion, chopped

Half a white cabbage, shredded finely

4 tablespoons mayonnaise

4 tablespoons salad cream

1 tablespoon soft brown sugar

Juice of 1 lemon

1 tablespoon Heinz ketchup

1 tablespoon Branston pickle

FOR THE DUMPLINGS

250g self-raising flour

Some freshly chopped parsley

500 ml sunflower vegetable oil

FOR THE SALAD

3 peppers – 1 red, 1 yellow, 1 green

10 cherry tomatoes

1 whole cucumber

2 ripe avocados

Assorted lettuce leaves, to serve

Sea salt and freshly ground black pepper

1 Clean and cut the chicken into portions. Mix together all the spices and seasonings from the garlic powder to the chilli and toss with the chicken pieces. Preheat the oven to 190°C/Gas 5 and cook the chicken for about 40 minutes, turning in the seasonings once or twice, until tender.

2 Make a coleslaw with the carrot, onion and cabbage, mixing together the mayonnaise, salad cream, sugar, ketchup, pickle and lemon juice. Season well.

3 Mix the flour with a teaspoon of salt, some pepper and the chopped parsley, then mix with some cold water to form a dough. Roll into balls for dumplings.

4 Fry in hot sunflower oil until cooked, then drain on kitchen towel.

5 Make a salad with the peppers, tomatoes, avocado and cucumber. Serve the chicken on lettuce leaves with the coleslaw, salad and dumplings alongside.

HENRY FILLOUX-BENNETT

Duo of Lobster and Langoustine Ravioli on Trifled Spinach and Sweet-potato Croutons with Seafood Bisque

2 leeks

4 carrots

2 onions

3 celery sticks

1 clove garlic

Olive oil, for frying

500 g fish bones

12 pink/black peppercorns

3 bay leaves

250 ml dry white wine

1 x 400 g can lobster bisque

200 g unsalted butter

200 ml double cream

1 live lobster, about 800g

2 live langoustines

25 ml brandy

1 packet wonton pastry sheets

250 g baby spinach

1 sweet potato

Garlic and truffle oil

1 Chop up leeks, carrot, onion, garlic and celery sticks and fry half in olive oil until golden brown. When browned, add fish bones, peppercorns, bay leaves, and 200 ml white wine. Cover with cold water, bring to the boil and simmer for 20 minutes.

2 Allow to stand for 10 minutes, then carefully strain through a fine sieve for fish stock.

3 Mix the stock with the bisque and return to the boil until reduced by half to a thickened sauce. Whisk in the butter, then half the cream.

4 Make the ravioli. Poach the lobster and langoustines in court bouillon for 6 minutes (see Basics, page 43). Shell the meat from the lobster and langoustines and finely chop.

5 Finely dice the remaining onion, celery, leek and garlic and pan-fry in more oil until soft but uncoloured. Deglaze with the brandy and remaining white wine and reduce until almost evaporated away. Add the remaining cream and bubble until thickened. Stir in the diced shellfish meat at the last minute.

6 Set aside to cool in the fridge. Lay out the wonton paper and brush around the edges with water. Spoon shellfish filling into the centre and place another wrapper on top, pressing down on the wet edges to seal.

7 Bring a pan of water to the boil then cook the raviolis in batches for about 3 minutes. Drain with a slotted spoon as you cook the remaining raviolis. Keep warm.

8 Serve with fried sweet potato and sautéed spinach that has been dressed with garlic and truffle oil.

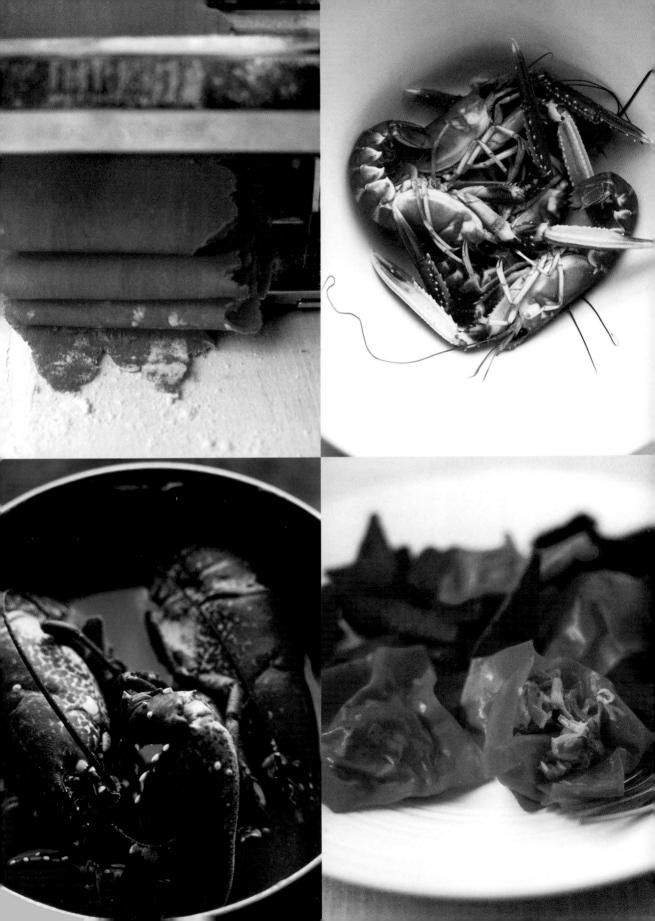

KELLIE CRESSWELL

Glazed Salmon with Honey, Mustard and Fresh Asparagus

250 g salmon fillet, cut in half
3 tablespoons honey
1 tablespoon wholegrain mustard
150 g asparagus spears
Olive oil
Fresh parsley

1 Preheat the oven to 220°C/Gas 7. Lightly oil frying pan and place over a medium heat. Season salmon and seal in frying pan. Remove from pan and place in ovenproof dish, then coat with honey and mustard glaze. Bake in the oven for about 10 minutes.
2 Meanwhile, blanch the asparagus in lightly salted boiling water for about 2 to 3 minutes, then plunge into iced water and drain again. Pat dry.
3 Heat a little oil in a heavy-based griddle pan and chargrill the asparagus until marked. Remove salmon from oven and place onto a warm plate, then pour over the honey mustard glaze and garnish with the asparagus. Sprinkle over some chopped fresh parsley.

'The best moment is being at the pass and seeing your food go out as it should be.' Kellie

SAM RAMPLIN

Sam's Yum Soup Selection

FOR THE TOM YUM SOUP:
2 lemon grass stalks, chopped
1 fresh red chilli, chopped
1 small knob fresh ginger, finely chopped
2 cloves garlic, crushed
2 fish stock cubes
2 stems Thai lime leaves
250 g shelled tiger prawns
125 g button mushrooms
1 small bunch fresh coriander
Juice of 1 lemon
Sea salt and freshly ground black pepper

FOR THE RICE:
200 ml coconut milk
125 g basmati rice
FOR THE STIR-FRY:
A little groundnut oil
6 baby corn cobs, halved
100 g shitake mushrooms, sliced
50 g canned bamboo shoots
Handful fresh mangetouts
1 teaspoon sugar
3 tablespoons soy sauce
1 clove garlic, crushed

1 Make the soup first. Fry the lemon grass, chillies, ginger and garlic in a little hot groundnut oil for 2 minutes. Add 600 ml of boiling water and stir in the fish stock cube until dissolved. Add the lime leaves to infuse. Add the prawns, mushrooms, and coriander and lemon juice. Simmer for 5 minutes.

2 Next make the coconut rice. Put the coconut milk into a pan with 300 ml of water. Stir in the rice, bring to the boil, then turn down the heat, cover and simmer very gently for 12 to 15 minutes. Allow to stand for 5 minutes, then stir to serve.

3 Make a stir-fry with all the stir-fry ingredients. Serve everything together – the soup in a bowl and the rice and stir-fry on a main dish.

'I feel now that I'm confident in the kitchen. I feel stronger. I've come so far.' Sam

SIMON GROSS

Leaning Tower of Pasta

500 g beef mince
Olive oil, for cooking
2 large mushrooms, chopped
1 onion, chopped
1 red pepper, cored and chopped
1 x 400 g can red kidney beans
1 large courgette, sliced
1 x 400 g can chopped tomatoes
150 ml red wine
1 x 350 g jar pasta sauce
500 g pack whole-wheat spaghetti
125 g chunk fresh Parmesan cheese, grated
Sea salt and ground black pepper

1 Fry the mince in a hot frying pan with some oil, stirring to break up. Then add the
chopped vegetables and cook for 5 more minutes. Stir in the kidney beans, courgette,
canned tomatoes, red wine and pasta sauce.
2 Season and bring to the boil, then simmer gently for about 20 minutes until cooked.
3 Boil the pasta according to pack instructions, then drain and toss with some more oil.
4 Serve the pasta with the sauce and Parmesan cheese sprinkled on top.

'My dream restaurant would be
contemporary but with a 1970's look.
You know, Moulin Rouge – red drapes,
velvet. Vaudeville is the word I'm
looking for.' Simon

STEIN SMART
Seafood Paella

25 g butter
2 to 3 tablespoons olive oil
1 onion, chopped
1 red pepper, cored and chopped
250 g paella rice (or Arborio risotto rice)
1 teaspoon ground turmeric
Half a teaspoon crushed saffron strands
2 cloves garlic, chopped
200 ml dry white wine
About 750 ml fish stock
About 1 kg mixture of raw prawns (in shells),
fresh mussels (in shells) and prepared squid
Sea salt and freshly ground black pepper

1 Heat the butter and a little oil in a large frying pan or wok, then gently fry the onions and pepper until softened. Stir in the rice and cook for about 4 minutes, then mix in the spices and garlic.
2 After a minute or so, add the wine and cook for 2 minutes, then add all the fish stock. Bring to the boil and simmer for 5 minutes.
3 Add the fish, in batches to get it all mixed in, and cook for about another 20 minutes or so, shaking the pan occasionally but not stirring it. The rice is cooked when it is slightly sticky and still a little moist. Check the seasoning and serve immediately.

'I was a bit nervous at first but when the adrenaline starts, the orders come in, and Jean-Christophe says they're picking us because they like us, something takes over.' Stein

TERRY MILLER

King Prawn Rockefeller

SERVES 4

3 shallots, finely chopped

40 g butter

1 x 75 cl bottle dry white wine

2 sprigs fresh tarragon, chopped

1 teaspoon English mustard

100 ml fish stock

200 ml béchamel sauce

25 g freshly grated Parmesan cheese

3 tablespoons double cream

A squeeze of fresh lemon juice

200 g baby-leaf spinach

8 large, cooked king prawns, shelled

2 cloves garlic, crushed

About 500 g potatoes, cooked and mashed, ideally Idaho potatoes

Tabasco sauce, to serve

125 g grated Cheddar cheese

A little chopped fresh parsley, to garnish

Sea salt and freshly ground black pepper

1 Sauté the shallots in 25 g of the butter until softened. Add the wine, tarragon and mustard and boil until reduced right down by half, then stir in the fish stock and béchamel sauce. Stir in the Parmesan and cream, then check the seasoning, adding lemon juice to taste. Set aside.

2 Pan-fry the spinach and garlic in the remaining butter until wilted and cooked. Then season and spoon into four warmed ovenproof oyster or scallop dishes.

3 Pipe the mashed potato around and sit 2 prawns on top of each dish. Shake a drop or two of Tabasco on top of each prawn, then coat with the sauce.

4 Sprinkle over the cheese. Preheat a grill until glowing and brown the dishes until bubbling and golden. Sprinkle with a little parsley and serve hot.

'The days of instant mashed potato are behind me.' Terry

'If I had to pay for this meal I would be
happy, but I probably wouldn't come back.'
Michel Roux

All anyone wants to know the next
morning is what went on in the shower
between Aaron and Sam. Did they, didn't
they? Not that there's much time to
speculate, since another sacking looms
and, again, the chefs will each have
to nominate a member of their team.

At roll call, Gary Rhodes admits he has
a problem, since all five trainees are now
performing well and there is no longer
an obvious weak link. Terry is among the
strongest, Sam is doing well, but Aaron
is out in front. Gary tells the team that
Aaron's reward for excellence will be to
eat in the restaurant that night. The
others will have to cover for him. 'He's
from your corner, Caroline,' says Gary.
'Simon, you've got to be there to help
and support Caroline.'

In the blue kitchen, Jean-Christophe
explains that he has to nominate
someone to go. He asks his strongest
team member to step forwards. Aby
moves at once. Jean-Christophe
challenges her. 'Why you?'

'I'm not the weakest,' she says.

Again, he invites the strongest to step
forwards. This time, it's Kellie. 'I was put
in at the deep end last night and I think I
was quite strong and quite confident,' she
says. Jean-Christophe plants a kiss on her
forehead. She will have the night off and
join Aaron in the restaurant for dinner.

One by one, the trainees sit down with
the chefs to explain why they want to
stay in Hell's Kitchen.

Terry believes he has been putting
a huge amount of effort into his work.
Gary Rhodes agrees. 'You have got a feel,
an understanding of how food should be
cooked,' he says. 'In terms of negatives,
you don't mingle and mix with the team.'

The two trainees struggling the most
have been Simon and Caroline. Off duty,
they're both popular with their team-
mates. Caroline has become the mother-
figure of the group. 'I've got nowt but
respect for her,' says Terry.

'She's fantastic,' says Aaron, 'quirky,
entertaining.'

Gary Rhodes has yet to be convinced.
'Can somebody please explain what
planet she's from?' Caroline enlightens
him. Mars, it would appear.

She reckons she should stay. 'I'm
definitely not the worst in the room,'
she says. 'I don't want to be nominated.'

'You wake up every morning with the
most fantastic, positive attitude,' Gary
Rhodes tells her, 'but then quite often
it doesn't go any further. The moment
we open the doors, panic sets in.'

Simon also wants to stay, but
acknowledges he has a lot to learn. 'I'm
now pushing it up a pace, I'm trying hard.'

Gary tells him he has one major

weakness. 'It goes in here,' he says, tapping his head, 'and straight out the other side.'

Sam, in the beginning one of the quietest members of the team, is becoming more confident with each passing day. Her cooking is impressive too. As for Aaron, his improved attitude – and his ability to cook the perfect scallop – have won his chef over. He has come a long way since Gary bawled him out during the first night's service. 'I thought we'd fall out. Now you're pleasing me,' says Gary.

The fact that both Sam and Aaron are in the chef's good books bodes well for their budding romance. Outside the kitchen, the pair are rarely apart. 'He makes you feel like a princess and you've never felt that about anybody in your life before,' Kellie observes.

Sam agrees. 'He's lovely. He's got the biggest heart.'

Jean-Christophe wants to know why Stein thinks he should stay. 'I want to win it,' he says. 'I've been here four days and I've come on immensely, so if you give me the chance I think I can progress even more. As long as I've given a hundred per cent that's all that matters.'

The chef loves his positive attitude but has one major problem. Stein is too excitable. 'You have got to relax and calm down. You've got a massive voice, you make the pans vibrate. Be less loud,' he says. Sound advice from a chef whose outburst a few nights before had caused every head to turn in the restaurant.

Kellie has consistently impressed Jean-Christophe. She's level-headed, hard-working, and she can cook. 'I think I give more than two hundred per cent,' she says. 'It's a marathon and I've got stamina.'

Her only weakness, he says, is that she asks too many questions. 'Work more by not giving anything away, but keep it inside you,' he says.

Gary thinks he should remain part of the blue team because he is a star. 'I'm passionate, I love food,' he says. 'I've got what it takes to be the champ.'

Jean-Christophe, though, has detected fear in Gary's eyes. 'It's like you're scared, not knowing where you are going,' he says.

Aby, her fingers covered in plasters, tells Jean-Christophe she is just starting to get the hang of things in the kitchen. He acknowledges that she has a positive attitude but says, 'You have got to slow down and listen.' he says.

'You've seen nothing yet,' she tells Jean-Christophe.

Aby, having fallen out with Jean-Christophe and infuriated Kellie, has also taken to sniping at the maître d'. 'I really don't like her,' she says.

The feeling is mutual. Laura says, 'I don't have much time for Aby. She rubs me up the wrong way. I would expect to see the contestants committed to their work and respectful to their chef, and I don't feel that from Aby.'

There's no doubt in Stein's mind about who should get the blue team nomination. 'Aby's the right person to go,' he says.

Red team trainee Simon admits he is worried. Caroline admits she should be. As for Rasta Gary, despite Jean-Christophe's reservations, he remains not-so-quietly confident. 'I think he knows a winner when he sees one,' he says.

As service gets under way, Gary Rhodes urges his team to do even better than the night before. He is less than confident, however. Without Aaron on starters, he knows Caroline is going to be at full stretch and confesses to Adam, his sous chef, that he has 'bad vibes'. 'Just take it slow,' Adam tells him.

Gary rolls his eyes. 'With this team, there's no other way.'

In the blue kitchen, Jean-Christophe wants to see his team – particularly Gary – pick up the pace. 'Express yourself, my friend. Be quick,' he tells him.

Both kitchens have good reason to be at their best. Among the celebrity diners is chef Michel Roux, who orders from the red menu, declaring Jean-Christophe's too complicated. 'There's so many bloody things going on,' he says. 'At least with Gary's it's straightforward and you know what you're going to get.'

Gary Rhodes, who counts Michel Roux among his heroes, is thrilled to get the check. Unfortunately, it is not a good night to be eating at Hell's Kitchen and, for the red team, things are falling apart fast . As Aaron relaxes in the restaurant, his team-mates are sweating. Caroline, struggling and failing to cover for him, pushes Gary to breaking point. 'Get the job done!' he screams at her.

In the blue kitchen, Jean-Christophe, who had started out in playful mood doing high kicks, is rapidly losing patience with Gary. 'Where is your mushroom gateau?' he says. He touches the plate. 'This is now cold.'

'I should have come in here as a musician, then maybe he would have been easy with me,' says Gary. 'But because I came in as a chef he might feel threatened.'

Stein is also struggling to keep pace with the checks. It's clear that everyone is feeling Kellie's absence. Chris, the blue team's sous chef, tells Stein to take time out in the courtyard. Stein does as he's told, but he's not happy to be sent out. 'Made me look half a pansy,' he complains.

For Michel Roux, Hell's Kitchen is a letdown. When he asks for salt and pepper it's clear all is not well. 'If I had to pay for this meal I would be happy,' he concedes, 'but I probably wouldn't come back. Put it that way.'

All in all, Gary Rhodes is having his most stressful night.

There is at least some consolation when the diners' verdict arrives. It's a red win with an overall score of eight out of ten. The blue kitchen has just five out of ten, a poor result. Jean-Christophe is despondent. His team has not performed well. 'We lost, that's it,' he says. 'You want to win, you get discipline.'

Without Kellie, Stein had buckled under pressure and Gary just hadn't been quick enough. 'I did my best,' he tells Jean-Christophe. When it comes to nominations, it's Gary facing the sack. Not that he seems to be overly concerned. 'I still believe in myself

and I don't think I'm going nowhere,' he says.

In the red kitchen, Gary Rhodes is reluctant to single out any of his trainees. 'This is more and more difficult as the days go by,' he says. 'I feel everybody has lifted their standard.' In the end, he nominates Caroline.

'I'm absolutely furious,' she says, maintaining a brave smile. 'I'm a very hard worker.'

She is, but it's her failure to listen that drives Gary Rhodes insane. 'All I get is, "Oh I'm sorry, I'm so sorry,"' he says. 'I'm sick and tired of hearing it.'

'I'm a useful person in that kitchen,' Caroline says. 'I'm not ready to go.'

Upstairs, in their living quarters, Aby is starting to feel that she's the outsider in her team. And Aby being Aby, she just can't keep it to herself. 'Where do I fit into this team?' she asks Stein. 'I've put myself out for you time and time again and I just get ignored. I get blanked. I do feel that you and I have a problem.'

Stein is probably the wrong person to tackle. Not prepared to mince his words, he says, 'I personally think you're an attention-seeker. You've been wrapped in cotton wool. Do you come from a middle-class family?'

She admits she does. That's it, then. The others, he says, are from the streets. 'We're no class,' Stein tells her.

'I'm the middle-class, stuck-up cow,' Aby complains later. 'The little runt, the one that sticks out, and that's fine. I'll have to keep taking it.'

While the blue team debates class issues, things are generally good among the reds, particularly where Aaron and Sam are concerned. They've been doing their best to enjoy the odd private moment together whenever possible. Not easy, with cameras following their every move. So far, they've enjoyed a few stolen moments in the shower room – a camera-free zone – one of the few places it's possible to have some privacy. Unless, that is, Stein happens to be in the cubicle next door.

He confides in Kellie and Aby that he'd heard things getting steamy between the

pair of them. 'The walls are only thin,' he says. 'It weren't full on, but it was all, "Oh baby, do you want it? Do you want it?"'

The blue trainees present themselves for roll call the following morning to find Jean-Christophe with the look of a man who has been pacing up and down the kitchen in a fury all night. He glowers at them. Sensing his mood, no one chances a cheery 'bonjour'.

Gary, whose lack of speed had infuriated the chef the night before, admits he may have messed up by failing to communicate with his team. On the other hand, he may just have been tired. Jean-Christophe doesn't want to hear it.

'The only thing I'm interested in is winning,' he says.

As the reds troop down from their living quarters to roll call, two members of the team are missing. Aaron and Sam, inadvertently delayed by a call of nature, perhaps, hurry to catch up. After a second winning night on the trot, the mood is decidedly upbeat. 'Quite phenomenal,' Gary Rhodes tells his troops. 'Something I could not have dreamed about.'

After dinner with Kellie in the restaurant the night before, Aaron has some positive news for his chef. 'Kellie said our food was superb,' he says.

Gary Rhodes is delighted. 'I'm lapping this up. This is what I want to hear.'

Both sets of trainees face a new challenge. They have 45 minutes to come up with a pasta dish, the most outstanding of which will appear as a special on the menu that night.

Eager to impress, they set to work.

In the blue kitchen, Kellie has produced a dish that scores on taste and texture, but loses marks because the prawns are overcooked. Aby's pasta is too crunchy.

When it comes to Gary, whose dish is designed to appeal to all tastes, Jean-Christophe is impressed. 'A meat-eater could eat it and feel nice, a vegetarian could eat it and feel nice, and you could have it with salad, potato, rice or whatever you want – bread,' says Gary.

Stein has opted for spaghetti bolognese with garlic bread. 'Not all arty-farty, just put together and slapped in a bowl. Something you sit down in front of the telly and eat,' was how he summed it up.

Jean-Christophe has a problem. Both dishes are excellent, scoring nine and a half points. He flings down his tea towel in exasperation. 'Now I've got a problem,' he says. Of Gary's effort, he says, 'Fantastic dish, very simple. Top notch.' Stein's is equally good. 'I have never put bolognese on the menu in my life, but this will match my standard and my style and my reputation.' It is impossible to decide between the two, so a coin is tossed. Stein's dish will be that night's special.

In the red kitchen, Gary Rhodes surveys his team's efforts. Caroline, already facing the sack, has pulled out all the stops with mushrooms and onions in a reduced cream sauce. 'Not a lot of mushroom happening there,' Gary says, prodding it with a fork. It's also lacking in seasoning. 'I'm not too keen on eating cold lumps of pasta,' he tells her. She scores four out of ten.

'So sad,' she says. 'He thought it needed seasoning. I didn't.'

She is by no means the worst. Aaron has cooked meatballs. Or rather, he hasn't. When Gary cuts into one, it's raw. 'This is called food-poisoning pasta, is it?' Aaron admits he ran out of time. 'Minus four,' is Gary's verdict.

Simon who, after a shaky start in the kitchen, has been showing signs of improvement, waits anxiously for Gary to inspect his dish. He has gone for an unusual combination of boiled ham in cream. 'What I decided to do was keep it simple, because there's no point in being too clever if you can't do it,' he says.

Gary wonders how many marks out of ten Simon would give his own dish. 'At least six for effort and commitment,' he replies.

Gary shakes his head in disbelief. 'Two out of ten.'

Terry, always one of the more promising trainees, if a little difficult for the others to understand at times, has cooked lobster with white wine, garlic, shallot, aniseed and asparagus. Gary gives him six out of ten.

Sam has produced ravioli filled with lobster, cream, cheese, garlic and seasoning. She also scores six. Gary decides the ravioli will be that night's special, much to Terry's disappointment. 'That's a bit unfair,' he says, 'I cooked the lobster and you've picked hers over mine.'

Gary has his reasons. The ravioli is easier to prepare, which means less pressure during service. In theory, at least.

As another night's service begins, each kitchen has prepared ten portions of their pasta special. Maître d' Laura sets about selling it to the customers.

TV presenter James Whale, tempted by Stein's spaghetti dish, wants to make sure it's up to scratch. Laura elaborates. 'It's homemade spaghetti with a bolognese sauce made with lots of red wine, rosemary and basil,' she says. Convinced, he orders it. Hours later, he is outside Hell's Kitchen, clutching a bottle of wine and complaining that he could have made a better bolognese out of a packet.

In the blue kitchen, Kellie is being driven round the bend by Aby's demands. As Aby barks orders, calling for this and that to be brought to her, Kellie realises that everything she is being asked for is already within her team-mate's reach. She complains to sous chef, Chris. 'She must be used to a butler,' she tells him.

It's all too much for the usually even-tempered Kellie. Screaming in frustration, she storms out of the kitchen, with Chris in pursuit. 'Is it me?' she says, slumping into a seat. Chris shakes his head. To Kellie's annoyance, Aby appears, keen to know what all the shouting is about. Or, as Kellie puts it, determined (again) to be the centre of attention.

In the red kitchen, Gary Rhodes peels off his top to show off an impressive six-pack. It's his birthday and, after two consecutive winning nights, he feels he is on a roll.

'This is our winning night,' he says. 'So much so I am getting sick and tired of winning. Do you understand?'

His good mood doesn't last, however. The checks are coming in fast – too fast for his liking. He tells Laura to slow things down. 'I've got ten covers here. I don't want to see another ten covers for ten minutes,' he tells her. 'I'm sure you've done it in your restaurant. Do it in my restaurant. *Slow down*.'

'Why is Gary so stressed out this evening?' says Laura. 'I think it's quite obvious. Everybody's chosen from his menu.'

Among the celebrity guests is pop star and classical musician, Myleene Klass. 'I think we've waited about an hour for our main course,' she says. 'It's fine, the wine is flowing and we're having a good time. But we are starting to waste away.'

As the checks pile up, there is confusion at the red kitchen pass. Gary's good humour evaporates. He looks for someone to take to task. Laura sashays into his sights.

'I am furious,' he tells her, his voice rising to a bellow. 'How many more checks are you going to take, because I'm going to tell you my kitchen is closed. This is getting ludicrous. *Ludicrous*.'

'That's it,' she says, 'finished. The whole restaurant has ordered.'

Gary glares at her. 'Kiss my backside, then.'

Things are not much better in the blue kitchen, where Gary – nominated for the sack because he can't seem to get a move on – is still operating at half-speed. Jean-Christophe pulls him up for presenting a goats' cheese starter that is already getting cold.

There are compliments and brickbats for the blue team. 'So many of the puddings were fantastic,' says Jean-Christophe. 'The steak was fabulous, but the sauce was like a cheap pizza topping.'

Gary Rhodes gives his team a diner's verdict on Sam's ravioli special. 'Tough and uninteresting and lacking in lobster,' he says.

The red team score five out of ten for quality of food. The blues do better with seven out of ten. 'I cannot understand why on earth the blue team get that,' says Gary. 'It makes my blood boil.' As Jean-Christophe congratulates his team, Gary shakes his head. 'As far as I'm concerned, this is a red-kitchen win,' he says.

Things are about to go even further downhill for the red team. Gary Rhodes will soon lose a trainee. With Caroline and Gary up for the sack, the votes have finally been cast and Caroline is going home. Despite her brave smile, she is, she says, gutted to be leaving. She senses there would be little point, however, in adopting Stein's tactics and chaining herself to a lampshade. For her, the Hell's Kitchen experience is over.

4 CLASSIC BRITISH FARE VERSUS JE NE SAIS QUOI

'With me you will eat with your eyes
first and then chew with your stomach.'

Jean-Christophe Novelli

It hasn't escaped anyone's notice how different the blue and red kitchens are in terms of cooking and presentation. Gary Rhodes prides himself on his classic British dishes and a menu that diners can take in at a glance. There is no place in the Rhodes kitchen for such culinary fripperies as flowers sculpted from root vegetables.

Jean-Christophe, however, has a more extravagant touch. A fussy, flamboyant, complicated touch. The blue team is convinced that more effort goes into their food, but the reds know that just because a dish looks neater on the plate it is no less challenging to create. Especially working to Gary's stricture that only perfection will do. Whether one menu is better than the other is surely a matter of taste. Unless you happen to be talking to the head chefs, that is.

'I think Gary is safe,' says Jean-Christophe. 'My menu is a lot more demanding.'

Gary disagrees. 'The only extra work that went into that menu was in the amount of words he uses to describe each dish. A lot of it is bullshit on a plate,' he says. He singles out a Novelli main course for special mention. 'Roast turbot with Devon cream curry

potatoes,' he says. 'Who gives a shit where the cream comes from?' He pulls a face. 'Spring garlic essence, minute "home fed" English mussels. Young river-cress oil and bean-sprout cress. That's *one* dish. That's a whole menu to me.'

There is a simple explanation. 'With me, you will eat with your eyes first and then chew with your stomach,' says Jean-Christophe.

Another dish has caught the Rhodes eye. 'Quick-fried English Channel sole fillet,' he says. 'I mean, the English Channel is filthy, dirty water. Who wants to eat that? Chorizo oil with jumbo asparagus, roast peppers. Sounds like greasy, dirty mud to me.'

Jean-Christophe is unmoved. 'We need to transmit what is inside a dish,' he insists.

'Please ask for extra bread to mop up the mess of your plate,' says Gary.

All in all, not impressed, then.

The trainees, having been given an extra hour in bed, arrive for roll call raring to go.

In the red kitchen, Gary praises his team. Terry says he feels that at last he is connecting with his cooking. 'You've got to get inside the meat, the turbot, the salmon, to know exactly how it's cooked. It's unbelievable,' he enthuses.

During the previous night's service, Gary Rhodes had done a bit of snooping on his blue kitchen rivals. In his view, the reds' consistent approach to their work is a distinct advantage. 'Consistency, in any walk of life, is what breeds success,' he tells the trainees. 'I believe we are stronger, tougher. I think we've got better-quality cooking.'

In the blue kitchen, Jean-Christophe tells his team that he may have pushed them too far the night before. 'Perhaps we did too many covers,' he says. 'Therefore, we're going to come back to some kind of exclusivity.'

His team is feeling positive. 'It's all fallen into place, which is making our lives easier,' Kellie tells him.

As the teams set to work, Jean-Christophe passes on some tips about cooking the perfect vegetables. 'Hot water, salt, vegetables in for two minutes, cold water, drain,' he says. 'There's nothing worse than a crunchy vegetable that's been kept in hot water.'

Kellie appears bemused. 'I've been giving them seven minutes,' she says.

Jean-Christophe staggers backwards. 'Seven minutes? It might take seven minutes to *grow* them …' The idea leaves him doubled up with mirth.

In the red kitchen, Simon, hard at work on the rhubarb and custard cheesecake, is finally managing to do something right. 'Gary's been a lot better with me today,' he says. 'He's been much more positive and he believes in me a lot more, which makes me feel so much better.'

'He's really turning the corner,' Gary says. 'There's a lot of potential in him. You know, he's an intelligent young man. He's got a great personality, lots of laughs – lots of headaches to go with it – but the great thing is to see somebody who came here with absolutely zero culinary knowledge starting to pick it up.'

In the blue kitchen, Kellie has noticed sediment in the bottom of a bottle of wine. 'Is it because it's cheap?' she wonders. Far from it, as it happens. It is around £35 a bottle. 'I thought it was three-quid cooking wine,' she says, shocked.

As service gets under way, Gary Rhodes, pleased with Simon's performance throughout the day, asks him to help Terry. It is to prove a major error as, at every turn, Simon falters and Terry, frustrated, complains. Gary can't understand it. He wants to knock some sense into Simon. 'I want to grab him and shake him and shake him until everything falls into place, because it's so jumbled up in that brain of his,' he says.

In the blue kitchen, meanwhile, Jean-Christophe spots a VIP guest; his rival head chef's wife. He beckons the maître d' and asks her to take something to the table with his compliments. She refuses. 'You know the rules,' she tells him. He does, but he's not about to abide by them. Once her back is turned, he takes Mrs Rhodes a carrot, carefully crafted into a flower. From the red kitchen pass, Gary Rhodes watches with contempt. 'Carrot flowers sent to my family from the blue kitchen,' he says. 'I can't wait until his family comes in. I'll come up with something: a parsnip tulip. See if they eat that.'

Aby is having a bad night on the desserts for the blue team. Her marzipan palm trees refuse to stay upright, toppling over en route from pass to table. She is beginning to lose her grip on reality. 'It feels like some weird dream,' she says, 'tearing round making marzipan trees and battling with a sex god.'

Her problems are nothing compared to those of the red kitchen, however, where Terry is rapidly losing his patience with Simon. Having busied himself preparing potatoes, Simon manages to ruin them by adding the wrong sauce to the dish. Terry then entrusts Simon to trim some asparagus for him. A simple enough task, but Simon hasn't quite grasped that when Terry told him to take an inch off the ends, an inch is what he meant. No more, no less.

The usually gentle Geordie, tutored in the Rhodes school of perfection, loses his rag. 'How much are you cutting off?' he says, appalled at the butchered stalks of asparagus on the chopping board. Simon, also at the end of his tether, throws up his hands in despair. 'Well, Terry, if it's not good enough, I won't help you. Do it yourself.'

It's an attitude that doesn't go down well with his head chef. 'Shut your mouth,' Gary tells him. 'Shut your mouth in my kitchen and don't speak like that. Do you understand? He said to take one inch off. Do as you're told – or if you don't like it, you know what you can do.'

Gary takes Simon outside. Moments later, Terry appears. 'You tried to f**k me up in there tonight,' he says, furious. As the pair begin to bicker, each blaming the other, Gary decides to intervene. He tells them he wants to see them working together without any hoo-ha the following night. Their task is to come up with a pre-starter, something the red kitchen can serve to everyone.

'Now get your heads together, guys,' he says. It does the trick. Their differences forgotten, they begin discussing croutons and cold soups.

In the restaurant, Laura finds half her time is spent taking orders and the other half apologising to diners. The complaints generally fall into two categories; there's something wrong with the food, or there's no food at all.

Those without anything to eat usually compensate by drinking. 'I have never seen so many drunk people in any restaurant,' says Laura. When Hell's Kitchen closes after two weeks of business, the diners will have got through 2,600 bottles of wine, around two bottles per head.

When the diners' verdicts come through, both kitchens have scored eight out of ten for quality, and an overall score of eight. It's a draw. The blue team whoop and shout, banging on the pass. Gary Rhodes is not happy. 'If anyone thinks they matched us tonight, it's a dream,' he tells his trainees, as the din next door continues. 'I'd rather lose than be equal to them. Listen to it. They are animals in there. No class, no style, no camaraderie.'

Upstairs, in the trainees' living quarters, Aaron and Sam celebrate in their own unique, loved-up style, ending up in bed together. Simon and Terry, their room-mates, do their best to ignore them. 'If they'd have started bonking, I probably would have gone mad,' Terry says. 'There's a place for that, and a time.'

Next morning, Sam wakes up and rushes straight to the bathroom where she throws up. She can't face roll call. Aaron does his best to cover for her, claiming a Chinese takeaway the night before has upset her stomach, but Gary Rhodes has his own theory. He suspects drinking on an empty stomach is behind Sam's sudden bout of sickness. The head chef goes to the living quarters, where Sam, buried under the duvet, promises to report to the kitchen in half an hour. When she finally does surface, she tells Aaron she won't be letting him get her drunk again. All the red trainees are still reeling from the blue kitchen's reaction to the diners' verdicts from the night before.

'They drew with us,' says Gary. 'and they're right to jump up and down because that's a big achievement for them. I think we're in a different league.'

'They're just common,' says Simon.

All the trainees are in for a stressful day. For the first time, a double sacking – one red team member, one blue – looms. They're all conscious that they may be spending their last few hours in Hell's Kitchen. Sam and Aaron agree that if they go before the end, they'll ask to stay in the same hotel. 'Write your number down for me,' says Aaron, 'just in case.'

No one wants to leave. In terms of cooking ability – or lack of it – Terry thinks Simon should be the one to go. Interestingly, Simon thinks it should be Terry. 'I think I've held the team together really well and contributed a lot,' says Simon.

'I don't deserve to be sacked because I'm still being who I am,' says Terry. 'I'm pushing myself to the limit.'

Sam also thinks Simon – the weakest in the kitchen, in her view – should leave. Aaron, keen to become a better cook, and get to know Sam better, is determined to stay until the end.

At blue roll call, Jean-Christophe tells his team he's convinced complaints about shards of eggshell in a starter the night before cost them dearly. It was still, however, his best night. Kellie agrees, suggesting the service in the restaurant may have let them down.

There is a new challenge for the teams. Both chefs want to measure just how much progress their trainees have made in the course of a week. They want them to have another go at the signature dishes they made when they first arrived at Hell's Kitchen.

The red team gets cracking. It's a far cry from Day One, when an atmosphere of mild chaos prevailed. As Gary Rhodes paces about, keeping an eye on them, the kitchen is practically an oasis of calm. 'I'm expecting some great improvement, OK?' he tells them. 'I want to see you all sweating a little bit.'

As the trainees line up with their signature dishes, Gary nods in approval. 'You can tell everything has been done with a little more class, a bit more style.'

Aaron, whose first attempt at sea bass, garnished with raw broccoli, had been less than successful, manages to impress the chef. Sam, unable to pronounce the name of her dish a week ago, achieves a better balance of flavours second time around. Gary moves on to Terry's King Prawn Rockefeller. One week on and Terry knows better than to insult his head chef with instant mashed potato. The chef's verdict: 'I can't stop eating it,' Gary tells him.

Simon's spaghetti bolognese is a vast improvement. 'That has come on so fast,' Gary tells him. 'I can eat this.'

It's Terry's Rockefeller that emerges the clear favourite for its just-right sauce, succulent prawns and mash.

In the blue kitchen, the trainee's efforts to recreate their signature dishes also draw praise from their chef. On the first day in Hell's

Kitchen, Kellie had cooked salmon – garnished with strawberries. She wasn't about to make the same mistake again. Jean-Christophe is impressed. 'The sauce is perfect,' he told her. 'It's actually quite original. Well done.' Gary, castigated for his chewy dumplings on Day One, has changed his technique. 'That is what I call a dumpling,' Jean-Christophe tells him.

Stein's paella, which started life as a mixture of undercooked prawns and overcooked rice, is pronounced colourful and tasty. Aby's first attempt at 'sexy chicken' had left the chef reaching for a glass of water to take away the taste. In the space of a week, however, she has learned how to cook to Jean-Christophe's exacting standards. 'Last time it was rough, seriously rough,' he tells her. 'The chicken is perfect, the sauce is sublime.'

They know, however, that despite the huge strides they have made, one of them will be leaving at the end of the night. Gary, who has already faced the sack once, does not want to be the one to leave. 'I've got the character to be a top chef,' he says. 'And I've got the skills to be a top chef.'

Stein is having too good a time to leave. 'I enjoy the lack of sleep, I enjoy working my knackers off, I enjoy not seeing my wife,' he says. 'I've never quit anything. I've got sacked a few times, I must admit.'

Kellie wants to keep learning. She has her sights set firmly on her own restaurant. And Aby wants time to prove that she's more than just the runt of the team, although she senses she may be on her way out. The night before, she started packing.

Back in the red kitchen, having paired Terry and Simon the night before, with disastrous consequences, Gary Rhodes is determined that all his trainees should learn to work together. He swaps the team around again and puts Terry and Simon on starters together.

In the blue kitchen, Jean-Christophe also shuffles his team, taking Aby off desserts. 'Tonight I'm doing main courses and the only thing I've learned in relation to that is how to season food,' she says, concerned.

Stein will be on starters with Jean-Christophe, a prospect that leaves the builder less than confident. 'It's all going to be pear-shaped,' he predicts. Sure enough, once service is under way, the blue kitchen struggles. Stein cannot get the hang of the starters. 'I can't take it in,' he says. 'I don't know what I'm doing.' Team-mate Gary does his best to calm him. 'You'll get used to it,' he says, but Stein is not convinced. He does his best to respond to the checks, but some of the food going out is less than perfect. 'I'll end up having a heart attack,' he says.

The maître d', Laura, returns two dishes to the pass. 'The tiger prawns are raw on both of them,' she tells Jean-Christophe, as Stein continues to buckle under the pressure. 'It's starting to piss me off,' he says.

'Stein is definitely lost,' remarks Jean-Christophe, as beads of sweat form on his trainee's furrowed brow. 'No map. No compass. Lost.'

Things are in a similar state in the red kitchen where Terry, like Stein, is working on starters for the first time. 'I'm feeling terrible, chef,' he tells Gary. 'I don't know what I'm doing.'

'You will,' Gary assures him.

While Stein continues to navigate without a compass, Terry is soon finding his way. 'I don't think there's anyone who catches on as quickly as he does,' says Gary. 'He was nervous as hell, panic stations, so the first few tables I'm running around like a headless chicken trying to show him. All of a sudden, he's picked it up. Perfect.'

In the blue kitchen Stein continues to sweat. 'I'm in a tiswas,' he tells his chef.

'It's a nightmare,' says Jean-Christophe, struggling to find the right expression to describe Stein. 'He is like a bloke with a pair of glasses with one ear,' he finally concludes.

Gary is doing better, but is still too slow for the chef's liking. 'He's good, he's detailed, he's passionate, he's emotional, but he has got to be faster,' says Jean-Christophe. 'Gary will never be Linford Christie. It's as simple as that.'

With service as smooth as it's ever likely to get for the red team, Gary Rhodes decides to give Simon a break from kitchen duties. He sends him into the restaurant to serve one of the tables. 'Just mince over, go on,' he tells him.

Simon, by now used to following Gary's instructions to the letter, does just that. As the celebrity diners crane their necks for a better look, Simon tosses greetings this way and that.

'Good evening, I'm your waiter this evening,' he announces. Gary, watching from the pass, grins at the sight of his trainee's antics. 'I'm proud of Simon,' says Gary. 'He has a new spirit and a new confidence.'

When Simon returns he's full of himself. 'They all knew my name,' he says, astonished.

'Do you think that's a giveaway?' says Gary, pointing at the trainee's name on his chef's whites.

With Simon otherwise occupied, Terry is left to his own devices on the starters. 'Looks superb,' says Gary, casting an eye over a pan of scallops. 'Terry is Number One in the kitchen for me. He's become almost the leader of the pack. It's incredible.'

There's no disguising who's Number One in the blue kitchen – it's Kellie. She has emerged as the one member of the team Jean-Christophe cannot afford to lose. 'Without Kellie, that's it. The team can close the doors,' he says.

Well into service, Stein still has the look of a pressure cooker with the lid about to come off. The seafood skewer he has been working hard to get right ends up on the floor. 'This is really getting on my tits,' he complains. Elsewhere, Gary, struggling to make fiddly desserts with his big hands, is having the kind of night he'd rather forget. Jean-Christophe has had enough. 'Two big elephants fighting about a small mouse,' is how he sums up the trainees. 'Come with me,' he says, leading the pair into the courtyard. 'There is nothing wrong, OK?' he tells them. 'There is no need to panic. Rather than give yourself a heart attack for no reason, just relax.'

When the diners' verdicts come in, the red kitchen is triumphant. They have served 46 covers – their highest figure to date. The diners are largely complimentary. 'The scallops were out of this world. The rhubarb cheesecake was superb,' Gary says.

In the blue kitchen, Jean-Christophe scans his diners' comments. Someone has complained that the lamb was tough.

The red kitchen's duck has also attracted criticism. 'The duck was cold and chewy and I'd have liked something green with it.' Gary Rhodes rolls his eyes. 'Well, I'll tell you what, I'll blow my nose on it next time.'

Nothing can dampen his mood because his team has scored nine out of ten – the highest yet. 'We are ahead, guys,' he tells the team to cheers. The blues trail by just half a point. 'Half a point is nothing,' Jean-Christophe tells the blues. 'Trust me.'

Despite their best performances to date, everyone is tense, knowing they are about to find out who will be leaving Hell's Kitchen. The red team lines up in front of the pass. Simon can barely contain himself as Angus Deayton relays the viewers' vote. Sam is safe. Delighted, she returns to the kitchen. Terry, too, still has his place on the team. It's between Simon and Aaron. 'You ain't seen the last of me!' Simon yells.

He's right. It's Aaron – in Gary Rhodes' view, shaping up into an excellent cook – who is going home. 'Oh my God,' says Simon, as it sinks in that he's staying.

Aaron appears staggered by the news. He tells Angus Deayton the whole Hell's Kitchen experience was a lot tougher than he had imagined, and tips Terry to win. What everyone wants to know, though, was what had really gone on between him and Sam in the shower.

'Everyone thought we'd gone for a shower together,' he says. 'Thanks guys, great thought, but it didn't happen.'

'You took separate showers?' says Angus Deayton, unconvinced.

'We went into separate shower rooms,' Aaron insists.

As they chat, at the far end of the restaurant in the blue kitchen, a drama is unfolding as things come to a head – again – between Aby and Jean-Christophe. There has been an uneasy truce between the pair since they clashed a few days before, and Aby's habit of answering back finally sends the chef into orbit.

'Just go, just f**k off,' he explodes. As Aby, close to tears, retreats, he says, 'She gets on my nerves. I want her out from my kitchen.'

Moments later, Aby joins her team-mates at the blue kitchen pass, to find out which of them will be leaving Hell's Kitchen that night. Stein is the first to hear he is safe. Kellie, to the undisguised joy of Jean-Christophe, is also staying. She whoops with delight and rushes back into the kitchen where the chef throws his arms around her. It's between Gary and Aby. After a tense few seconds, Aby learns that she will be the one to leave. She nods, apparently relieved, perhaps aware that her final contretemps with Jean-Christophe had signalled the end of the line anyway.

As she returns to the kitchen to say goodbye to her team-mates, Sam and Simon lean across the hatch that separates the two kitchens to wish her well. Jean-Christophe, busy at the pass, keeps his back to her.

'We just had a huge blowout,' she tells Angus Deayton, blinking back tears. 'We don't mesh well.' She is shocked at the language unleashed on her by Jean-Christophe. 'He owes me a big, fat apology,' she says.

'The only thing I regret is that I had to tell a woman to F.O.,' he says, 'because that is not my manner.'

He makes no secret of his delight at Aby's dismissal. 'I'd like to thank every single one who voted from my heart,' he says. 'I'd just had enough. I couldn't stand any more. I just wanted her to go.'

As for Aby, her love affair with the fiery chef is well and truly over. 'He's gorgeous, but he f**king knows it,' she says. Tipping Kellie to win, she confesses that Hell's Kitchen has been a trying experience.

'It *is* hell. Childbirth would be easier.'

5 IF YOU CAN'T STAND THE CHEF GET OUT OF THE KITCHEN

'It's your reputation on the line. Let's not serve second-rate food.' Gary Rhodes

With Aby gone, things settle down in the blue kitchen. Not for long, however. Soon Stein, who has already shown signs of crumbling under the pressure of service, will fall foul of Jean-Christophe, with disastrous results. As a new day dawns, though, they're on good form and the blues have every confidence that they are in the hands of the best chef.

'It's definitely the fun kitchen,' says Stein.

'He definitely loves us,' says Gary, although he admits he only catches about seventy per cent of everything his chef says.

'The way he teaches us is another level completely,' says Kellie. 'And to allow us to be ourselves is a good thing.'

Not surprisingly, the red team, having also bonded with their chef, believe the Gary Rhodes approach is the right one.

'I would say Gary is a better leader, a better teacher, because he's got so much discipline,' says Simon, who has experienced more of it than most.

'His philosophy in the kitchen is quality, not quantity,' says Sam.

'His passion comes through,' says Simon. 'The need to be best.'

'He's just not taking any crap,' says Terry. 'If you've overcooked the salmon by thirty seconds, he'll know.'

Gary Rhodes senses that his kitchen has the upper hand. According to his team, the blues are an undisciplined bunch, given to falling out with one another. Their laissez-faire attitude will, he predicts, be their downfall.

'In the blue kitchen, it's do what you want to do,' he says. 'As long as the grub gets on the plate, who cares?' The easy-going, fun-loving, laid-back blues would never have survived under Gary's strict regime. 'I'd have shown them the door,' he says.

Discipline isn't everything, however, as the red kitchen discovers once service is under way. Gary Rhodes decides – foolishly, perhaps, with hindsight – to put Simon in charge of the pass. 'It all got a bit out of hand,' he says.

In the blue kitchen, Jean-Christophe puts Kellie in charge. She takes to it as if she has been doing it all her life.

Meanwhile, Gary Rhodes is increasingly perturbed at the manner in which his kitchen's food is being presented. 'It all went a bit pear-shaped,' he says.

In an effort to get things back on track he takes control and orders his team to slow down. He doesn't want the food thrown together; he urges them to take their time and get it right. It's a restaurant, not a burger bar, he reminds them. 'Everybody is now going to wait,' he says. 'And I don't care how long they have to wait.'

So, those unlucky diners who have ordered from the red menu wait. And wait. And wait. Among the celebrity guests are actors David Tennant and Richard Wilson. They harangue Laura, who goes to Gary to ask how much longer the main courses will be. He is not in the mood for polite conversation. 'I can't give you a time. I'm not a magician,' he says.

As the food continues to arrive at the pass cold, burned, and generally below the chef's exacting standards, he calls a halt and closes the kitchen. 'Right, that's it, I've had enough,' he says. 'I'm not sending anything else. This is a waste of time. It's second-rate, not good enough.'

It's left to Laura to explain to a restaurant full of hungry people why they won't be getting anything to eat.

'We've been waiting an hour for a main course and we've just been told it's not going to happen,' says David Tennant. Richard Wilson vows never to return to Hell's Kitchen.

'If something goes wrong backstage when I'm with the Royal Ballet we get out there and we improvise,' says Wayne Sleep, infuriated that Gary Rhodes will not take any more checks.

'If Gary has just run up the white flag because he feels his people are under pressure, I think that's letting the side down, I really do,' says Christine Hamilton.

One diner goes to the pass to find out why the service has come to an abrupt halt. 'I'm not prepared to serve substandard food,' Gary says.

Laura takes matters into her own hands and appeals to Jean-Christophe to fill the breach as Gary watches in disbelief. 'Look at what she's doing,' he says, as the rival chef promises to do what he can. While Gary seethes, Jean-Christophe leaves his kitchen to serve one of the red kitchen's disappointed tables.

There are no surprises when the diners' verdict appears. Gary's decision to close the kitchen early means that of the 42 covers

that came in, 28 were not served. Their overall score is just four out of ten.

For the blue kitchen, however, there is praise. 'Overall, the food was fantastic with an explosion of colour,' Jean-Christophe tells his troops. It is their night.

Gary is angry and frustrated. 'We handed it to them,' he says, complaining to Laura that the rival kitchen cannot possibly have fed forty diners. 'Are you telling me they fed everybody by eleven p.m.?' he asks.

Laura, unperturbed, assures him they did. 'Garbage,' he says.

With a win under their belts, the blue team has drawn level with the reds and, with the scores at five-all, they have every reason to be cheerful. Upstairs, in the living quarters, however, team spirit is sinking fast. When Stein wonders aloud who might be next to go Gary jumps in with both feet. 'I think it's you,' he tells Stein. 'I think it's me and Kellie in the final.'

At roll call the following morning, Jean-Christophe poses much the same question, keen to know which member of the team ranks strongest and which weakest. 'I think we're all on the same level, chef,' Kellie says. 'There's not a weakness between any of us three.' Gary, wisely, decides to keep the thoughts he'd been happy to express the night before to himself.

In the red kitchen, despite a bad night, the team is on form. Gary Rhodes wants to know their feelings about his decision to close the kitchen midway through service the night before.

'I learned something last night,' says Terry. 'It's no use serving food that's not right.'

Sam agrees. 'There's no way food should go out if it's not up to scratch,' she says.

Gary tells them it's their reputation on the line. 'Let's not serve second-rate food.'

Among the guests in the restaurant are members of the trainees' families, all bursting with pride. Service begins well for both kitchens but, as the night progresses and the checks start to pile up, the blue kitchen starts to come apart at the seams.

As Jean-Christophe keeps the pressure on, calling out checks, confusion descends on Gary, who's doing desserts. Stein, described by his chef as a man without a compass, looks utterly lost as he tries to keep pace with the main-course orders. He also appears to be on a short fuse.

One by one, the trainees' relatives come to the pass. Terry is in tears at the sight of his wife, Linda. The pair embrace. 'I love you, I love you,' she tells him, showering him with kisses.

An ear-splitting shriek cuts through the restaurant. It is Kellie's mum, Christine, approaching the blue kitchen, arms outstretched. 'Go girl, go! Kellie, Kellie, Kellie!' she says. Kellie wipes away a tear. 'Now you know where I get my gob from,' she says.

All the trainees are elated at the sight of their families. The red kitchen is on a high. 'It's a fine old night we're having here,' says Gary Rhodes. 'It's bloody phenomenal.'

The blue kitchen, meanwhile, is beginning to slide into crisis. Maître d' Laura does her best to find out if Jean-Christophe is taking more orders. 'I've got five more tables and they need to order in the next twenty-five minutes. I need an answer,' she tells him. Jean-Christophe shrugs. Laura, losing patience, says, 'OK, if you want to behave like a child, behave like a child.'

At the red kitchen pass, she explains that Jean-Christophe is not speaking to her and, in a neat reversal of the night before, Gary offers to handle all the remaining orders.

As the pressure mounts, blue trainee Gary has had enough. When he suggests Jean-Christophe closes the kitchen, the chef fails to respond. 'I hate it when I try my hardest and I don't get respect,' says Gary. 'I don't need attitude. I'm doing my best.' Even as Kellie is urging him to keep going, he's decided enough is enough. 'I'm quitting,' he says, disappearing into the courtyard.

When Kellie speaks to Jean-Christophe she gets the same silent treatment that has driven Gary to leave. She backs off but Stein steps in. 'Is he not talking to you?' Kellie, keen to keep what's left of the team together, shrugs it off.

As sous chef Chris approaches, Stein waves a serving spoon at him. 'He's being ignorant and there's no need,' he says.

Kellie says, 'Don't you dare lose your temper.'

While it's fast becoming the kitchen from hell for the blues, things could hardly be better for the reds. 'This is nothing but Pleasure Kitchen,' crows Gary Rhodes.

Jean-Christophe has ventured into the restaurant to apologise to the diners he failed to serve, among them Gail Porter. 'It's a nightmare,' he tells her.

In the kitchen, Stein remains dangerously close to losing his temper. 'When I talk to someone I expect an answer back, even if it's bollocks,' he tells Chris. 'Why don't you talk to him and ask him to stop being ignorant?'

Chris, who knows trouble when he sees it – and isn't about to make things worse by speaking to Jean-Christophe – urges Stein to go outside and cool off.

In the red kitchen, sous chef Adam, sensing drama, clocks his departure. 'I think Stein has just walked out,' he says.

Outside, Stein and Gary continue to complain about their chef who, just a few days earlier, they had agreed was a diamond geezer. Stein is ready to go back into the kitchen and flatten Jean-Christophe, but Kellie pleads for calm. The chef is having a bad night, simple as that. 'He's pissed off with himself,' she says.

'So talk to us properly,' Gary yells. '*Without* getting pissed off.'

Gary is not prepared to return to the kitchen. Stein is, but it's a bad move. Sparks fly almost at once.

'Have the vegetables been done?' he asks Jean-Christophe.

'It's burned,' the chef tells him.

Stein, ready to spontaneously combust, says, 'Please don't ignore me, chef.'

Jean-Christophe, puzzled, looks up. Stein,

infuriated, says, 'Please don't ignore me. Even if you tell me to shut up, please don't ignore me. I just asked you a question.'

'You can't see it's burned, no?' says the chef.

Stein turns on him. 'F**k you. *F**k you*,' he yells, stomping out of the kitchen for the second time in the space of a few minutes.

Kellie, still doing her best to calm Gary, sees Stein approaching. 'He won't talk to me like that again,' he says. Kellie, appalled, suggests the pair of them go upstairs and take a cold shower. Meanwhile, she returns to the kitchen to carry on cooking. Jean-Christophe has also had enough. 'I'll leave you in charge,' he tells Kellie, heading off. 'By the way – well done.'

With the chef's praise ringing in her ear, Kellie works on, unaware that by doing so she's risking the wrath of Stein. 'The only reason I lost my temper is because the chef ignored Kellie,' he says. 'And it looks like she's rubbed my nose in it by staying down there.'

All round, it has been a bad night for the blue kitchen. A walkout involving two-thirds of the team and the chef, a near punch-up and several hungry, dissatisfied diners.

'I had overdone fish, underdone vegetables and it was . . . er, lovely. Just the way I like it,' was how one diner sums up his night.

When the diners' verdict comes in, predictably it's good news for the red kitchen, with an overall score of nine out of ten, which puts them back in the lead. 'Stand back, stand back,' says Gary Rhodes, beaming with pride. 'Number of covers, thirty-seven. Number of people not served – zero. Potatoes, out of this world, garden salad was fresh and amazing. That came from Uri Geller.' A cheer goes up from his team. 'I don't know why I'm so calm because inside I'm boiling over,' he says. 'It's amazing. I can't thank you all enough.'

Upstairs, in the living quarters, as soon as Kellie is through the door Stein turns on her. 'He blanked you and I stood up for you,' he complains, 'and then you stay there.'

'I knew this was going to happen,' Kellie says.

'I felt you were disloyal to me,' Stein says.

Both Gary and Stein sense that Kellie is the chef's favourite and they don't like it. Stein grumbles to the red team. 'Kellie will win this. Absolute certainty. At morning roll call, it's all, "*Oh, Kellie, you're such a star.*" Soon as me and Gary say anything, he cuts us off.'

Terry says, 'You can't take it out on Kellie, though.'

Stein is willing to make a fresh start with his chef in the morning but Jean-Christophe has already decided that Stein's tantrum, coupled with a threat of violence, cannot be tolerated. As the others report for roll call, Stein packs and prepares to make a low-key exit from Hell's Kitchen.

'No one has ever mistreated me or disrespected me in the kitchen in the last twenty-five years. He is the only one,' says Jean-Christophe. 'As far as I'm concerned, I was there to help him to become a winner but, when it came to the point of losing respect, I'm sorry, there is nothing I can do. He had to go.'

As Stein leaves, his sole regret appears to be having defended Kellie the night before. 'I've come out for nothing,' he says. His respect for his chef, however, remains intact. 'I absolutely love him to death,' he says. 'I think he's a legend.'

DESSERTS

RED MENU
GARY RHODES

Bread and Butter Pudding

SERVES 6

1 x 400 g loaf sliced white bread, crusts cut off
Some unsalted butter, softened
1 vanilla pod
500 ml double cream
150 ml milk
6 egg yolks
125 g caster sugar plus extra for topping
75 g sultanas
75 g raisins
Caster sugar, for the caramelised topping

1 Preheat the oven to 180°C/Gas 4. Split the vanilla pod and place in a saucepan with the cream and milk and bring just to the boil. While it is heating, whisk together the egg yolks and caster sugar in a bowl. Allow the hot creamy mix to cool a little, then strain it on to the egg yolks, stirring all the time. You now have the custard.
2 Butter the bread, cut into triangular quarters or halves, and arrange in a medium-sized ovenproof dish in three layers, sprinkling the fruit between two layers and leaving the top clear. Now pour over the warm custard, lightly pressing the bread to help it soak in, and leave it to stand for at least 20 to 30 minutes before cooking to ensure that the bread absorbs all the custard.
3 The pudding can be prepared to this stage several hours in advance and cooked when needed. Place the dish in a roasting tray three-quarters filled with warm water and bake for 20 to 30 minutes until the pudding begins to set. Don't overcook it or the custard will scramble.
4 Remove the pudding from the water bath, sprinkle it liberally with caster sugar and glaze under the grill on a medium heat or with a cook's blowtorch to a crunchy golden finish. When glazing, the sugar dissolves and caramelises, and you may find that the corners of the bread begin to burn. This helps the flavour, giving a bittersweet taste that mellows when it is eaten with the rich custard.

Crisp Thin Apple Tart with Bramley Apple Sorbet

MAKES 1 X 20 CM TART TO SERVE 4

1 sheet of ready-rolled puff pastry

2 or 3 Granny Smith apples, peeled, cored and cut into 6

2 teaspoons caster sugar

2 tablespoons apricot jam

2 tablespoons water

FOR THE APPLE SORBET:

6 Granny Smith or Bramley apples, peeled, cored and roughly chopped

300 ml sweet cider

50 g to 100 g caster sugar

1 Make the sorbet first. Mix together the apples, cider and 50 g of sugar in a saucepan. Bring to a simmer and cook until the apples are tender (about 10 minutes).

2 Drain off the cooking liquor and boil to reduce it by half in another pan.

3 Blitz the apples and reduced liquor in a blender or food processor to a purée. Taste for sweetness – if too tart add extra sugar to taste.

4 Leave to cool, then churn in an ice-cream machine. Scoop into a freezer-proof container and freeze until required. Thaw 10 minutes before scooping.

5 To make the tarts, preheat the oven to 190°C/Gas 5. Roll out the pastry sheet a little thinner and cut out a 20 cm round. Lay the pastry onto a baking tray lined with nonstick parchment and leave to rest in the fridge for 10 minutes.

6 Cut the apples into slices and arrange them on top of the pastry disk from left to right until you have filled the tart. Sprinkle with the caster sugar.

7 Bake for approximately 15 to 20 minutes until the pastry is crisp and the apples have started to colour.

8 Boil the apricot jam with the water and brush each tart to give a glazed finish.

Rhubarb and Custard Cheesecake

MAKES ONE CHEESECAKE TO SERVE 6 TO 8

FOR THE BASE:
250 g digestive biscuits
120 g butter, melted

FOR THE RHUBARB CUSTARD:
450 g rhubarb, cut into rough 1 cm pieces
plus 250 g extra for topping
200 g light soft brown sugar
Juice of 1 lemon

2 or 3 drops grenadine, for colour, optional
3 leaves of gelatine, soaked in cold water
(or 2 sachets powdered gelatine)
450 g cream cheese
250 ml ready-made instant custard, chilled
100 ml double cream, lightly whipped
3 tablespoons caster sugar

1 Make the base. Crush the digestive biscuits into fine crumbs in a food processor.
Stir in the melted butter. Press the mix into the base of a 22 cm loose-bottomed cake
tin, and chill to set.
2 Soak the gelatine leaves in cold water until floppy, then drain, squeezing out excess
liquid. For powdered gelatine, mix with some cold water in a cup until spongy.
3 Put the 450 g rhubarb pieces and soft light brown sugar in a saucepan. Cook over
a medium heat until thick and mushy, stirring occasionally. Add the lemon juice and
liquidise to a smooth purée. Add a few drops of grenadine for colour, if liked. Pour the
rhubarb purée into a bowl and stir in the soaked gelatine until completely melted.
4 Put the cream cheese and custard in a food processor and blend until smooth.
Add the rhubarb purée and continue to blend until thoroughly mixed. Transfer the
mix to a large bowl and fold in the whipped cream. Pour the cream on to the biscuit
base and level the top to a smooth finish. Chill for 2 to 3 hours until set.
5 Meanwhile, cut the remaining rhubarb into 2 cm sticks and cook gently in a
saucepan with the 3 tablespoons of sugar for about 10 minutes until the rhubarb
becomes tender. Leave to cool.
6 To serve the cheesecake, warm a small knife in a bowl of hot water and run it
around the edge of the cheesecake and the tin to release it; the base will now push
comfortably from beneath. Divide the cheesecake into wedges and top with the
stewed rhubarb. Alternatively, make rhubarb strips (see below) for a decoration.

RHUBARB STRIPS

Slice the rhubarb lengthways into very thin strips – a mandoline can be used for this.
Lay the strips on a baking tray lined with parchment paper. Sprinkle lightly with caster
sugar and dry out in the oven at its lowest temperature setting for up to 12 hours.

Glazed Lemon Tart with Lemon Yogurt Sorbet and Fresh Strawberries

MAKES 1 X 24 CM TART TO SERVE 8
250 g sweet dessert pastry, thawed if frozen
FOR THE FILLING:
8 eggs
350 g caster sugar
300 ml double cream
4 lemons, juice from all, finely grated zest from 2
Icing sugar, to dust
Fresh strawberries to serve

1 Preheat the oven to 180° C/Gas 4 and lightly grease a 24 cm loose-bottomed flan tin or a plain ring at least 2 cm deep, placed on a baking sheet.
2 Roll out the pastry thinly and lift into the flan tin or ring with a rolling pin. Press well into the sides and trim the top allowing a little overhang. Fill with baking parchment and baking beans, then bake blind for 20 minutes, removing the beans after 15 minutes.
3 Mix together the eggs and caster sugar until smooth, then pour on the cream and mix in the lemon juice and zest.
4 Pour into the cooked flan case and bake in the preheated oven for 30 to 40 minutes until the tart is just set. Remove from the oven and allow to cool. Dust lightly with icing sugar to serve with the lemon yogurt sorbet (see below).

LEMON YOGURT SORBET

MAKES JUST OVER 1 LITRE
250 g caster sugar
900 ml unsweetened natural yogurt
8 tablespoons lemon juice
grated zest of 4 lemons

1 Heat the sugar with 500 ml of water until dissolved, then cool.
2 Mix the syrup with the remaining ingredients and churn in an ice-cream machine until smooth.
3 Scoop into a freezer-proof container and freeze until required. Thaw 10 minutes before scooping.

Almond Cake with Rhubarb Sorbet

MAKES 16 LITTLE CAKES

100 g unsalted butter plus extra, softened for greasing

115 g caster sugar

125 g ground almonds

1 teaspoon baking powder

25 g plain flour plus extra for moulds

25 g crumbled digestive biscuits

3 eggs

Half a teaspoon vanilla extract mixed with 120ml stock syrup (see Basics, page 175)

1 Grease and line little cake moulds or small tartlet tins, about 5 cm diameter, with softened butter and flour, shaking out excess.

2 Preheat the oven to 180 °C/Gas 4. Cream together the butter and sugar until light and fluffy.

3 Sieve together the flour and baking powder, then add the almonds and biscuits.

4 Stir into the creamed butter and sugar, then add the eggs one at a time, until the mix is smooth. Divide between the greased moulds.

5 Cook for 6 minutes, until they start to come away from the edges. Allow to cool slightly, then brush or pour the syrup onto each tart. Serve warm with scoops of rhubarb sorbet, below.

RHUBARB SORBET

MAKES ABOUT 1 LITRE TO SERVE 6 TO 8

650 g new seasons rhubarb cut into 2 cm dice

225 g caster sugar

Juice of 1 lemon

120 g liquid glucose

1 Place all ingredients into a pan and bring slowly to a simmer.

2 Simmer with a lid on for 10 minutes until the fruits are nicely puréed

3 Spoon into a liquidiser and blitz until very smooth.

4 Pass through a fine sieve, cool and churn in a machine.

Warm Soft Chocolate Pudding with White Chocolate Cream

MAKES 6 MOULDS

250 g butter, plus extra softened for greasing

4 teaspoons flour, sieved, plus more for the moulds

250 g dark chocolate, chopped

4 eggs, plus 4 extra yolks

120 g caster sugar

1 Grease six ramekins, about 120 ml capacity, with soft butter and place in the fridge until set. Grease again, then flour the mould and tap off any excess.

2 Melt the chocolate and butter over a bain-marie to 70°C (very hot but not boiling), stirring slowly and continuously.

3 Beat the eggs and yolks with the sugar in a heatproof bowl over a pan of gently simmering water to 37°C (hand-hot).

4 Remove from the heat and stir in the melted buttery chocolate, then fold in the sieved flour.

5 Fill the moulds three-quarters full and leave to rest for 15 minutes while you preheat the oven to 180°C/Gas 4. Place the moulds on a baking tray and bake for 8 to 9 minutes until crusty on top. Serve straight from the oven.

WHITE CHOCOLATE CREAM

SERVES 6

1 tablespoon liquid glucose

100 g white chocolate, chopped

250 ml whipping cream

2 medium egg yolks

A pinch of salt

1 Heat 2 tablespoons of water and the glucose to the boil in a medium-sized pan. Remove from the heat and stir in the chocolate, working until smooth.

2 Allow to cool for 2 minutes, mix in the yolks and salt, then cool.

3 Whisk the cream to soft floppy peaks and fold in. Scrape into a serving bowl, cover with clingfilm and chill until required.

BLUE MENU
JEAN-CHRISTOPHE NOVELLI

Passion Fruit and Mango Parfait

SERVES 16

250g caster sugar
5 large free-range egg yolks
2 ripe mangoes
4 ripe passion fruits, halved
2 teaspoons orange-flower water
2 large free-range egg whites
1 teaspoon fresh lemon juice
300 ml double cream

1 Dissolve 150 g sugar in 100ml boiling water and boil for 2 minutes. In a large heatproof bowl and using a hand-held electric whisk, beat the yolks until pale yellow and creamy, then gradually pour in the hot syrup, whisking as you pour. Continue whisking for 5 minutes until cool and thickened.
2 Peel the mangoes and cut off the flesh, then purée in a food processor with the orange-flower water and pulp from the passion fruit. Rub through a sieve with the back of a ladle. Mix with the sweet egg-yolk mixture.
3 Whisk together the egg whites with a squeeze of lemon juice until forming firm, but not dry, peaks. Then beat in the remaining sugar until you have a firm, glossy foam. Whip the cream until softly stiff.
4 The three mixtures should be all the same consistency, approximately. Simply fold them all together and scoop into 2 nonstick metal loaf tins about 1 litre capacity.
5 Freeze until solid, then cover and store. It will keep for up to 1 month. When ready to serve, dip the tin briefly in a bowl of hot water. Rub a table knife around the outside and shake out onto a platter. Serve in slices with more sliced mango, or pawpaw or a selection of summer fruits.

Bitter Chocolate Fondant with White Chocolate Sorbet

MAKES 6 TO 8

190 g dark bitter chocolate, at least 58% cocoa solids

190 g butter

4 eggs, separated

100 g caster sugar

20 g flour, sifted

Dark chocolate leaves, to serve

FOR THE SORBET:

100 g white chocolate

400 ml stock syrup (see Basics, page 175)

100 ml espresso-strength hot coffee

20 g liquid glucose

200 ml water

1 To make the fondants, break up the dark chocolate and place in a heatproof bowl, with the butter, over a pan of gently simmering water. Heat until melted, stirring occasionally.

2 Whisk together the egg yolks and sugar until light and fluffy, then fold in the flour. Mix in the melted chocolate-butter mixture.

3 Whisk the egg whites until forming soft peaks and gently fold into the chocolate mixture. Spoon into 6 to 8 greased metal moulds about 100 ml capacity and chill until ready to bake.

4 Heat the oven to 180°C/Gas 4. Place the moulds on a baking tray and bake for about 10 minutes until risen. Demould by running a table knife around the sides of the moulds and upend onto dessert plates. Serve with scoops of the sorbet and dark chocolate leaves, if liked.

5 To make the sorbet, melt the white chocolate in a heatproof bowl over a pan of gently simmering water. Don't overheat, as white chocolate can seize (become a think, lumpy mass) easily.

6 Heat the stock syrup with the hot coffee and slowly mix into the chocolate with the liquid glucose and the water.

7 Cool, then churn in an ice-cream machine until frozen. Scoop out into a freezer-proof container and freeze until required. Then thaw for 10 minutes or so until ready to scoop.

Strawberry Mirror

MAKES 6

300 g ripe strawberries, hulled

60 g unsalted butter, softened

2 egg yolks

2 egg whites

25 g caster sugar

90 ml double cream

1 sponge flan base

FOR THE MIRROR TOP:

6 tablespoons stock syrup (see Basics, page 175)

Half a leaf of gelatine

1 Hull the strawberries, then whiz to a fine purée in a blender. Rub through
a sieve and reserve 4 tablespoons for the top.

2 Place the remaining purée, butter and egg yolks into a saucepan and heat
gently until hot, but well below boiling over, 60°C on a thermometer. Take care
not to over cook the yolks.

3 Remove from the heat and cool completely.

4 Whisk the egg whites to soft peaks and whisk in the sugar to a meringue.
Then fold this into the strawberry mixture. Lightly beat the cream to soft peaks
and fold in also.

5 Cut off the rim of the flan case, then split the sponge base in half. Using metal
cutters about 12 cm diameter and 6 to 7 cm deep, cut out 6 sponge bases.

6 Lightly grease the metal cutters and place on a flat tray, lined with nonstick
baking parchment. Press in the sponge rounds and spoon in the mousse mixture.
Chill until set.

7 Meanwhile, soak the gelatine leaf in cold water until floppy. Remove and drain.
Heat the reserved strawberry purée and syrup until hot and stir in the gelatine until
dissolved. Allow to cool, then pour over the mousses, ensuring no bubbles form.
If they do, then pierce with a cocktail stick. Chill until firm.

8 Demould by running around the inside with thin table knife. Serve with fresh
strawberries to accompany.

Caramelised Granny Smith Apples Tatin with Vanilla Ice Cream

SERVES 2

2 apples, Braeburn or Granny Smith

50 g honey

80 g caster sugar

2 circles puff pastry, rolled to approximately 15cm

2 star anise

1 vanilla pod, cut in half

25 g butter

1 Heat the oven to 190°C/Gas 5. Peel and core the apples and trim to a neat shape. Line two small metal moulds about 10 cm diameter with discs of nonstick paper.

2 Heat the honey and sugar until dissolved, then raise the heat and cook to a golden caramel. Pour the caramel into the moulds. Press a star anise and half vanilla pod into each mould, then put the trimmed apples on top.

3 Press and mould the pastry discs around the apples and bake for about 15 minutes until the pastry is golden and crisp and the apples just tender.

4 Carefully turn the tatins upside down and demould onto dessert plates. Remove the papers, dust with icing sugar and serve with vanilla ice cream.

Coconut and Malibu Soufflés

MAKES 6

200 ml carton of creamed coconut

70 g sugar

1 teaspoon cornflour

1 tablespoon Malibu

30 g melted butter

About 50 g finely grated dark chocolate, to dust

3 egg whites

40g caster sugar

1 Boil together the creamed coconut and 25 g of the sugar until it is the consistency of syrupy jam (if you have a sugar thermometer this should reach 120°C). Remove from the heat and beat in the cornflour and Malibu.

2 Grease six medium-sized ramekins with the butter, then coat evenly in the grated chocolate. Heat the oven to 180°C/Gas 4.

3 Whisk the egg whites until forming soft peaks, then whisk in the sugar until thick and glossy. Fold the meringue into the coconut and divide between the ramekins, levelling the top with the back of a table knife.

4 Place the ramekins on a baking sheet and bake for about 12 minutes until risen and golden on top. Serve immediately.

'The secret of a good soufflé? If it's still rising after two minutes, it's perfect.'
Jean-Christophe

Pannacotta with Bitter Orange Peel in Grand Marnier Caramel

MAKES 6
4 sheets gelatine (12.5 g)
450 ml double cream
220 ml whole milk
100 g sugar
1 vanilla pod
Bitter orange peel in Grand Marnier caramel, see below

Put the gelatine in a bowl with enough cold water to cover and leave to soak for 5 minutes or until it becomes soft and pliable.

Meanwhile, put the cream and milk in a saucepan over medium heat and stir in the sugar until it dissolves. Heat the liquid just until small bubbles appear around the edge: do not let the liquid boil.

Turn off the heat. Use your hands to squeeze all the water from the soft gelatine. Add it to the simmering liquid and stir until it dissolves.

Split the vanilla pod and use the tip of the knife to scrape out the seeds, then add the seeds and pod to the pan. Cover the pan and leave the mixture to infuse for 30 minutes.

After 30 minutes, remove the vanilla pod from the liquid. Rinse 6 150 ml ramekins and put them on a baking sheet that will fit in your fridge. Equally divide the vanilla-flavoured mixture between the ramekins and leave them until completely cool. Cover the ramekins and chill for at least 3 hours until the pannacottas are set, but still slightly wobbly.

To serve, run a knife around the edge of each ramekin, then place a serving plate on top, top surface down. Invert the plate and ramekin, giving a firm shake halfway over. If the pannacotta hasn't dropped onto the plate, dip the base of the ramekin in a sink of hot water and repeat the process. Serve with orange peel in Grand Marnier caramel spooned over. (Or, use the mixed berry sauce on page 165.)

BITTER ORANGE PEEL IN GRAND MARNIER CARAMEL

SERVES 6

2 oranges

300 ml water

75 g caster sugar

175 ml Grand Marnier or other orange-flavoured liqueur

1 Cut each orange in half from top to bottom, then cut each half into quarters. Use a small knife to remove the orange flesh from each segment (this can be used in a salad or juiced) and cut away all but the thinnest layer of white pith. Use a vegetable peeler or sharp knife to slice the peel into thin strips. Continue until all the peel is sliced; set aside.

2 Put the orange peel in a pan of boiling water and blanch for 15 seconds, then drain and immediately tip into a bowl of iced water to stop the cooking. When cool, drain well and put in a heatproof bowl.

3 Put the water and sugar in a saucepan over a high heat and stir until the sugar dissolves. Bring to the boil, without stirring, and boil until the syrup turns an even golden brown. Use a pastry brush to remove splashes on the inside of the pan.

4 When the caramel is golden brown, remove the pan from the heat and stir in the Grand Marnier. If any of the caramel solidifies, return the pan to a low heat and stir until it melts.

5 Pour the caramel over the orange strips. Leave to cool completely, then cover and chill until required. (Any leftover orange peel and syrup can be spooned over vanilla or chocolate ice cream. Or try it with the almond ice cream on page 172.)

Hazelnut Meringues with Sweet Vanilla Cream and Mixed Berry Sauce

SERVES 6

60 g blanched hazelnut

3 medium egg whites, at room temperature

200 g caster sugar

2 teaspoons cornflour

1 teaspoon lemon juice

Half a teaspoon vanilla essence

FOR THE SWEET VANILLA CREAM:

250 ml double cream

Half a teaspoon vanilla extract

2 to 3 tablespoons icing sugar

FOR THE MIXED BERRY SAUCE:

200 g strawberries

200 g raspberries

200 g blackberries

100 g caster sugar, or to taste

1 tablespoon freshly squeezed orange juice

Finely grated rind of 1 orange

1 To make the vanilla cream, beat the double cream and vanilla together until soft, floppy peaks form. Sift over 2 tablespoons of icing sugar and fold it in. Taste and add an extra tablespoon of sugar if you would like it thicker. Cover with clingfilm and chill for up to a day.

2 To toast the hazelnuts, put them in a dry frying pan over a medium heat and stir for 3 to 5 minutes until they just turn light golden brown. Immediately tip them out of the pan. Leave to cool for a few minutes, then finely chop, but do not chop to a powder; set aside.

3 To make the meringues, preheat the oven to 140°C/Gas 1 and line a baking sheet with a silicone baking mat.

4 Put the egg whites in a bowl and whisk until stiff peaks form. Slowly beat in the sugar, one third at a time, until the meringue is stiff and glossy. Sift over the cornflour, add the lemon juice and vanilla and quickly beat in. Add the chopped hazelnuts to the bowl and fold them in.

5 Spoon the meringue into 6 equal mounds, about 8.5 cm across, on the baking sheet and bake for 40 to 50 minutes until they are lightly crisp on the outside, but not coloured; they should still be soft inside. Transfer the meringues to a wire rack and leave to cool completely. (These will keep fresh in an airtight tin for up to 3 days.)

6 Meanwhile, to make the sauce, hull the strawberries. Set aside about 50 g of each berry, then put the remainder in a saucepan over a medium-high heat with the sugar and orange juice. Stir to dissolve the sugar and break down the fruit, then bring to the boil without stirring.

7 Transfer the berries and liquid to a blender or food processor and blitz. Strain through a fine sieve into a bowl, using a rubber spatula to work the berries through the sieve. Stir in the orange rind, then the reserved berries. Cover and chill until required.

8 To serve, place a meringue in the middle of each plate. Top with a dollop of the vanilla cream, then spoon the fruit and purée over.

Sweet Sherry Syllabub with Spiced Shortbread Stars

SERVES 4 TO 6; MAKES ABOUT 30 BISCUITS
1 lemon
120 ml sweet sherry, such as Bristol Cream
75 g caster sugar
300 ml double cream
FOR THE SPICED SHORTBREAD BISCUITS:
200 g butter, at room temperature
100 g caster sugar, plus extra for the baking sheet
300 g plain flour, plus extra for rolling
1 teaspoon ground mixed spice
A pinch of salt

The shortbread biscuits can be made up to 4 days in advance or frozen for 2 months.
1 Put the butter in a bowl and, using an electric mixer, beat until soft and smooth. Add the sugar and continue beating until creamed. Sift in the flour, mixed spice and salt and mix until a soft dough comes together; if it remains 'flaky' use your hands to pat the dough together. Wrap in clingfilm and chill for at least an hour.
2 Meanwhile, preheat the oven to 160°C/Gas 3 and lightly sprinkle 2 baking sheets with caster sugar. Roll out the dough on a very lightly floured surface until it is 5 mm thick. Use a star-shaped cutter to stamp out about 30 biscuits, re-rolling the trimmings as necessary, but avoid overhandling.
3 Place the biscuits on the baking sheets and bake for 15 to 20 minutes until they turn pale golden. Use a palette knife to transfer the biscuits to a cooling rack, sprinkle very lightly with extra caster sugar and leave to cool completely. The biscuits will become firm as they cool. Store in an airtight container.
4 To make the syllabub, finely grate the rind from the lemon and put it in a large bowl. Firmly rub the lemon back and forth on the work surface, then squeeze 1 ½ tablespoons of juice and add it to the bowl with the rind. Stir in the sherry and sugar, making sure the sugar is dissolved. Cover the bowl and set aside for the flavours to blend for at least 2 hours, but ideally overnight.
5 At least 2 hours before serving, add the cream to the bowl with the liquid and, using an electric mixer or stick blender, beat until soft peaks form. Spoon the syllabub into 4 or 6 wine glasses or glass bowls. Cover with clingfilm and chill until ready to serve.

Fresh Fruit Skewers with Black and White Dips

SERVES 4 TO 6

A colourful selection of fresh seasonal fruit, such as apples, bananas, blackberries, Cape gooseberries, kiwifruit, oranges, mangoes, raspberries, starfruit and strawberries
Lemon juice

FOR THE RICH CHOCOLATE-BRANDY DIP:

2 tablespoons golden syrup

4 tablespoons double cream

50 g plain or dark chocolate, to taste, chopped

10 g unsalted butter

1 tablespoon brandy

FOR THE CRÈME FRAÎCHE DIP:

175 ml crème fraîche

1 teaspoon vanilla extract

2 tablespoons icing sugar, or to taste

1 To make the chocolate-brandy dip, melt the golden syrup in the double cream in a small saucepan over a high heat, stirring, then bring to the boil. Remove the pan from the heat, add the chocolate and stir until it melts. Stir in the butter and brandy and continue stirring until the dip becomes glossy with a consistency of lightly whipped cream; set aside. This can be served warm or chilled.

2 To make the crème fraîche dip, beat the crème fraîche and vanilla together, then sift over the icing sugar and stir until blended. Taste and add extra sugar, if desired. Cover and chill until required.

3 Make the selection of fruit by what is looking best in the shops, aiming for a colourful selection. Prepare the fruit as close as possible before serving: quarter and core the apples, then cut them into thin slices and brush with lemon juice; peel and cut the bananas into bite-size slices and brush with lemon juice; pull back the papery white layers of the Cape gooseberries; cut the kiwifruit into bite-size wedges; peel the oranges, separate into wedges and use a small serrated knife to remove all the membranes; peel the mangoes, remove the flesh from around the stone and cut into bite-size pieces; rinse the raspberries and pat dry; hull the strawberries, and leave them whole.

4 To serve, give each guest a small bowl of each dip with a selection of fruit on a plate. Serve with long, thin fondue forks or bamboo skewers for dipping the fruit in each dip.

Pears Poached in Champagne with Brandy Chocolate Glaze, Toasted Almonds and Glazed Pear Crisps

SERVES 6

1 bottle (750 ml) champagne or other sparkling wine
200 g caster sugar
1 vanilla pod, split
1 cinnamon stick
10 black peppercorns, lightly crushed

7.5 cm strip lemon peel, with all white pith removed
6 ripe pears, such as Bosc or Comice
60 g flaked almond
Rich chocolate-brandy dip, warm (see page 168)
12 glazed pear crisps, see right

1 Put the wine, sugar, vanilla, cinnamon, peppercorns and lemon peel in a saucepan over medium-high heat, stirring to dissolve the sugar. Bring to the boil, then reduce the heat and leave to simmer while preparing the pears.

2 Peel each pear, then cut them in half, quarter and remove the cores. Immediately drop the pear quarters into the simmering wine and poach for 8 to 12 minutes until just tender; the exact time depends on size, variety and ripeness.

3 Use a slotted spoon to transfer the pears to a heatproof bowl and set aside. Bring the poaching liquid to the boil and boil until reduced by half. Pour the syrup over the pears and set aside until completely cooked, then cover and chill until required.

4 Meanwhile, toast the almonds. Put the almonds in a dry frying pan over medium–high heat and stir for about 5 minutes until they just start to turn golden brown. Immediately tip them out of the pan.

5 To serve, spoon the pears into a glass bowl or cocktail glass. Very lightly drizzle with the chocolate glaze and sprinkle with toasted almonds. Serve with the glazed pear crisps.

GLAZED PEAR CRISPS

MAKES AT LEAST 24

100 g caster sugar

1 or 2 pears, such as Conference, well rinsed and dried

1 Preheat the oven to 110°C/Gas ¼ and line 1 or 2 baking sheets with a silicone baking mat. Place the sugar on a plate and spread out.

2 Cut one pear in half and place one half cut side down on the work surface. Using a mandoline, cut long, ultra-thin slices, without bothering to remove the core or seeds. If you don't have a mandoline, use a wide vegetable peeler or sharp knife to cut slices as thin as possible.

3 Place the pear slices in the sugar and lightly coat on both sides, then transfer them to the baking sheet(s) in a single layer. Continue slicing the pears until you have 24 slices.

4 Bake the pear slices for 1 hour. Using tongs, carefully turn the slices over and continue baking for a further 1 to 2 hours, until the slices are crisp and just starting to turn golden brown.

5 Transfer the pear slices to a wire rack and leave them to cool completely: they will become crisper as they cool. Store in an airtight container for up to 3 days.

Baked Figs with Pinot Noir Sauce and Almond Ice Cream

SERVES 6

6 to 9 figs, depending on size

400 ml Pinot Noir

60 g caster sugar

Finely grated rind of 1 orange

3 tablespoons orange juice

Almond ice cream, see below

1 Preheat the oven to 180°C/Gas 4. Cut the figs in half from top to bottom. Place the Pinot Noir, sugar and orange rind and juice in a small roasting tin or a flameproof dish that will hold the figs upright in a single layer, and stir until the sugar dissolves. Add the figs, cut sides up, and spoon some of the wine mixture over. Bake for 8 to 12 minutes, depending on size and ripeness, until the figs are just tender, basting once after 5 minutes.

2 Using a slotted spoon, remove the figs from the liquid and set aside to cool in a heatproof bowl that will hold them upright.

3 Transfer the liquid to a saucepan and bring to the boil; boil until reduced to about 175 ml. Spoon the syrup over the figs and leave them to cool completely.

4 To serve, place 2 or 3 fig halves on a plate and drizzle a little of the syrup over. Add a scoop of almond ice cream alongside (see, page 174) .

ALMOND ICE CREAM

MAKES ABOUT 750 ML

3 large egg yolks
100 g caster sugar
350 ml full-fat milk

Half a teaspoon almond extract
250 ml double cream
175 g blanched almonds, toasted and finely chopped

1 Beat the egg yolks and sugar together in a heatproof bowl until thick and creamy and the sugar dissolves. Put the milk in a saucepan and heat just until bubbles appear around the edge: do not boil.

2 Slowly whisk in the hot milk, beating constantly. Return the mixture to the rinsed pan and simmer over a very low heat, stirring constantly, for about 10 minutes or until it is thick enough to coat the back of a wooden spoon and hold the mark if you run your finger through the custard on the spoon.

3 Remove the custard from the heat and stir in the almond extract. Leave the mixture to cool, then cover the surface with clingfilm and chill. (The mixture can be left in the fridge for up to a day at this point.)

4 Whip the cream until soft peaks form, then fold the cream into the chilled custard. Pour into an ice-cream machine and freeze according to the manufacturer's instructions, adding the chopped almonds when it is about half frozen. If you don't have an ice-cream machine, set the freezer to its coldest setting several hours in advance. Freeze the ice cream in a shallow freezer-proof bowl until it sets around the edge. Tip the ice cream into a bowl and beat until smooth. Return it to the freezer and repeat the beating process twice more at hourly intervals.

5 Transfer the ice cream to the fridge 10 minutes before serving to soften.

DESSERTS
BASICS

STOCK SYRUP

MAKES ABOUT 700 ML SYRUP

275 g caster sugar

1 lemon

1 vanilla pod, optional

1 Dissolve the sugar in a saucepan with 500 ml boiling water and bring to the boil.
2 Using a swivel vegetable peeler, cut off thin slices of zest from the lemon and add to the syrup together with the vanilla pod, if liked. Leave to infuse for at least 24 hours.
3 This can be stored without decanting in a screw-topped jar or bottle. Best kept chilled.

APPLE CRISPS

MAKES ABOUT 15 CRISPS

1 Granny Smith apple

150 ml stock syrup (see above)

1 vanilla pod

1 Core the apple neatly then slice thinly. Place in a pan with the syrup and vanilla pod. Poach gently for a minute or so then remove from the syrup, drain and lay out in a single layer on a large roasting tray.
2 Dry out in an oven on the very lowest temperature possible. When crisp, remove to an airtight container.

ALMOND TUILES

MAKES AROUND 24
4 large free-range egg whites
50 g caster sugar
25 g plain flour
250 g ground almonds

1 Whisk the egg whites to froth, not foam. Beat in the sugar, flour and ground almonds.
2 Heat the oven to 180°C/Gas 4. Place a nonstick baking parchment on a large metal baking sheet.
3 Spread a small teaspoonful of mixture as flat as you can to a neat round using a small palette knife, allowing room for expansion.
4 Bake in batches of 5 or 6 until golden brown round the edges – this takes around 7 minutes. Wait for a few seconds before scooping the tuiles off the sheet onto a wire tray, where they will become light and crisp.
5 For curled tuiles, press them lightly round a thin rolling pin one at a time, holding down with a tea towel. For tuiles baskets press them over a small orange or upturned spoon. Store in an airtight container.

'It's almost like the culinary World Cup –
England versus France.' Gary Rhodes

Stein's departure has left the remaining members of the blue team subdued so Jean-Christophe, aware that events have affected morale, is keen to get his trainees back on track. He is certain the eventual winner of *Hell's Kitchen* will come from his team.

'Don't give up, the two of you,' he says. 'And don't leave the kitchen, please.'

Gary's discussion with Stein the night before about Kellie being the favourite of the group is still preying on his mind. He decides to share his concerns with his chef. 'I feel there might be a little bias in the group at times,' he says. 'I don't know if you have a better relationship with the ladies ...'

Jean-Christophe insists there are no favourites. 'I love you,' he tells Gary. 'Give me a kiss.' Gary, not entirely comfortable with the idea of kissing a man, backs away. Jean-Christophe, however, used to his trainees doing as they're told, won't take no for an answer. 'I want a kiss,' he insists. As Gary begins to explain his reluctance, Jean-Christophe silences him with a manly embrace.

With just a few days left for their teams to prove themselves, both chefs can sense things becoming more intense. 'It's almost like the culinary World Cup,' says Gary Rhodes. 'England versus France.'

'I've got to think as a coach. The

match starts now. You want to play and score,' says Jean-Christophe.

'There's no extra-time in the kitchen. Once the diners' verdict is in, that's it,' adds Gary Rhodes.

As the football analogies take hold, David Ginola runs onto the pitch ... or rather arrives in the restaurant.

Being shorthanded seems to suit the blue kitchen. The red team detects a new, conscientious atmosphere among their rivals. 'They're certainly getting their heads down,' Simon says. 'Before, they were very noisy.'

Kellie confirms that the blue kitchen has become a more peaceful place. 'We've got our own little space and our own little areas,' she says. 'There's no one getting in the way.'

In the red kitchen, Simon is telling sous chef Adam that, once *Hell's Kitchen* is over, he plans to invite him and Gary Rhodes round for afternoon tea. Adam appears dubious but Simon is already planning a menu. 'Tea and scones,' he says. 'I'll cook.' Adam and Gary Rhodes exchange concerned looks.

Gary Rhodes is getting the perfection he wants from his team. For once Laura is not having to fend off complaints. Jennie Bond, who ordered from the red menu, is full of praise. 'It was excellent. I can't fault it, really,' she says. The sole dissenting voice is that of David Ginola, concerned that all the shouting going on in Jean-Christophe's kitchen is giving the French a bad name. When Laura passes this on, the chef raises an eyebrow. 'Did he like the food?'

'Yes, he did. Very much,' says Laura.

It is all Jean-Christophe cares about.

The diners' verdicts reveal that the red kitchen has served 46 covers. Gary Rhodes relays some of the comments to his team. 'Scallops – delicious and succulent. Risotto – fantastic. The texture was superb.'

In the blue kitchen, there is praise too for Jean-Christophe's team. 'Mushroom pancake was just divine – so light it almost disappeared.' The blues have scored a respectable six out of ten but the red team has a staggering nine out of ten. They now lead 7–5. Just one more win will put them beyond the reach of the blue team.

The blues can't understand it. 'Was it my meat?' says Kellie. 'My fish?' Jean-Christophe thinks it was simply the fact they did fewer covers, but Gary suspects Kellie let the side down. 'She better sort herself out,' he says.

With just five trainees left, and another sacking on the cards, the competition is getting tougher every day.

Terry cannot quite believe how far he has come. 'I'm a local lad from Newcastle,' he says. 'To get this close is absolutely phenomenal. Spot on. I'm not the brightest person in the world but I've given a hundred and fifty per cent.'

Sam, too, has made huge strides since she first arrived in Hell's Kitchen. 'I'm learning different things every day,' she says. Simon is barely recognisable from the trainee who once inadvertently put salt instead of sugar in a lemon sorbet. 'I'm confident about winning against Sam and Terry,' he says. 'They're great people but they don't have any zest.'

Both chefs have a new challenge for their teams. They want the trainees to come up with a new signature dish. One from each kitchen will end up as a special on that night's menu.

In the blue kitchen, Kellie decides on turbot with tomato and layers of wild mushrooms, pan-fried in garlic. After four minutes in the oven it should be perfectly cooked, but when Jean-Christophe goes to taste it, the fish is raw. Kellie can't understand it.

Her team-mate Gary has opted for lamb cutlets with yam and tomatoes. Jean-Christophe is in raptures over the sauce. Gary's dish will be that night's special.

As both trainees begin the preparation for service, Kellie suspects the failure of her turbot was down to sabotage. She complains that Gary turned down the oven. Gary denies it, but Kellie is certain. 'You're a poor loser,' he tells her. 'Just accept that I won and that's it.'

'He's playing a game,' she says.

The two continue to be at odds as service approaches. When Jean-Christophe compliments Gary on his tomato sauce, Kellie interjects. 'I made that,' she says.

'I told her how to do it,' Gary snaps back.

There's more bickering when Gary prepares some potato for Kellie. It's off. 'This is shit,' Jean-Christophe tells her, tasting it.

'Gary tasted it and said it was lovely,' she replies.

'I couldn't taste nothing bad,' says Gary. 'Taste your own dishes.'

In the red kitchen, Simon has decided on duck in an orange sauce as his new signature dish. Sam is making a beef stew with herb dumplings, classic English cooking guaranteed to appeal to Gary Rhodes. 'That's really got my taste buds rolling over,' he says. Terry has also opted for something quintessentially British: lamb with redcurrants, a twist of mint, and some rosemary.

As they get cracking, Gary raises an eyebrow when he sees Simon using orange squash as the base for his sauce. When it comes to tasting all three dishes, it's the sauce that detracts from an otherwise excellent dish. 'It's a bit gooey, isn't it?' Simon says. 'A bit too syrupy.'

Gary is impressed with Terry's lamb dish. 'Wonderful and tender. You have the lamb, the rosemary, and the sweetness of the redcurrant behind it. That's a very, very nice combination,' he tells him.

Sam's stew, served in an individual pan, with the dumplings on the side, is also impressive. 'Beautiful presentation,' says the chef. 'You've got so much flavour going on there.'

He's torn as to which one should go on the menu. In the end, 'Simon's Duckie' wins the day. 'That's going to be a sellout,' says Gary.

It's a crucial service for Gary Rhodes and the red trainees. One more win and his team will be overall winners. Jean-Christophe, however, is determined to stop them in their tracks. He buoys up the blues. 'Don't forget you are very good, all right? We speak, we don't shout. We love each other and we do the job.'

Among the diners in Hell's Kitchen, are Aaron, Caroline, Henry and Aby, whose ankle-skimming red dress lets everyone know which kitchen she now supports. Gary Rhodes is cock-a-hoop. All four decide to order from Gary Rhodes' menu – until Henry has a crisis of confidence. He asks Laura to let Jean-Christophe know he is rooting for the blue kitchen. 'Aby has ordered from the other kitchen,' Laura tells the chef.

'That's fantastic,' he says, with a wicked smile. 'Now we have no need to poison her!'

Among the celebrity guests is racing pundit John McCririck. Having been tipped off that he could well go hungry, he arrives clutching a food hamper, much to the annoyance of both chefs. Before his table's starters have a chance to arrive from the red kitchen, he and his wife tuck into the potted shrimp and salmon they have brought with them.

Both specials are proving a popular addition to the regular menu. In the red kitchen, though, disaster strikes when Simon takes his eye off his 'duckie' just long enough to burn the last two portions. 'It's my fault, it's my fault,' he wails, tipping what's left of his dish into the bin. 'Please send my apologies,' he tells Laura.

Gary Rhodes has every confidence in his team, however. So much so, that he and Adam are about to leave them to it. 'I thought, let's put some pressure on the guys,' he says. 'They've got to do it. And we were having such a good evening I didn't think anything could go wrong.' Brave words, but ones he would end up having to swallow later, all the same.

As Gary Rhodes mingles with the diners, Laura waits at the red-kitchen pass. And waits. 'There are customers out there a bit concerned they're not getting fed,' she says. One customer in particular is not prepared to wait any longer. Singer H, formerly with the pop group Steps, takes matters into his own hands and approaches the pass. The duck, ruined by Simon, had been destined for his table.

'Where's our main course?' he says.

'It's coming,' Terry says.

'We ordered an hour and a half ago,' says H. 'We ordered duck.'

'That's coming,' Terry says.

'We were told it was burned.'

'That was me, I take the blame,' Simon says.

'I'll be back later with marks out of ten,' the singer threatens.

In the blue kitchen, Kellie gleefully witnesses the exchange. 'He's the second one to complain,' she says.

As their head chef continues to chat with the diners, the red team struggles on. Two steaks and a salmon come back, all less well done than the customers had wanted. Terry is starting to lose his rag. 'Do the whole table again,' he tells the others.

Gary Rhodes appears just as chaos is beginning to descend. 'What happened?' he says. Terry points the finger at Sam and Simon; too busy running up to the pass when they should have been doing other things, in his view.

Front of house, Laura glides among the tables, dealing with queries and complaints.

'I don't think some of the diners at Hell's Kitchen are used to gastronomic restaurants,' she says, tactfully. 'I think they find the menus a little daunting.'

Jean-Christophe suspects that at least some of the complaints are fuelled by alcohol. 'Some celebrities complain,' he says, 'but I've noticed some of the celebrities were a little bit pissed.'

'We're in the kind of industry where people can complain if food is not up to standard,' says Gary Rhodes. 'Or, where they don't get anything to eat.'

In John McCririck's case, it was a bit of both. Having polished off his own starter as well as one from the red kitchen, racing's most eccentric character blusters at Gary Rhodes. 'The potato was like Smash,' he says.

Gary's usual charm and courtesy where diners are concerned vanishes. 'I bet one hundred per cent that you haven't got a clue what you're talking about,' he says.

While he's at the pass, McCririck decides to have a go at Jean-Christophe too. 'Lucky I didn't order from your kitchen. I'd have ended up poisoned,' he says.

Jean-Christophe is not in the mood. 'I don't like you,' he says. 'I think you're a pig.'

'I'm a customer, you should look after me!'

'I don't give a f**k,' the chef tells him.

Having promised to return with marks out of ten for his food, H does just that, giving the red team a consistent minus ten for everything, and dragging down their overall score. Gary Rhodes reads some of the diners' comments to his team. 'Simon's duck – congratulations on a beautiful dish. You should be proud of your creation. Cheesecake

– too soft, no crunch. Rhubarb undercooked.'

In the blue kitchen, Jean-Christophe reports to his team. 'Lamb disappointing, completely overpowered by cheese and spice – Henry.' He looks baffled. 'Henry?' It's the verdict of his former trainee. 'Oh no!'

Gary reads on. 'Scallops fine and fillet steak good. Pastry needs improvement. That's John McCririck.'

The blue team has the edge, with an overall score of nine out of ten. Kellie jumps for joy. The red kitchen trails by just one point. 'That just makes my blood boil,' says Gary Rhodes. 'It's rubbish. Pure, pure bullshit.'

With Stein having already been sacked from the blue kitchen, the Jean-Christophe's remaining trainees are off the hook. One of the red team is about to be dismissed, however. Sam, Simon and Terry line up in front of the pass to hear the results of the viewers' vote.

Angus Deayton tells Terry he is safe. It is between Sam and Simon, who relieves the tension by bursting into song.

'The person the public have decided should leave Hell's Kitchen tonight is . . . Simon.'

He strides through the restaurant, arms raised in triumph. 'You haven't seen the last of me yet,' he promises.

Of his blue-kitchen rivals, he rolls his eyes. 'They're like *EastEnders* gone wrong,' he says, but tips Kellie to win. 'She's a real person,' he says. 'What you see is what you get. She's a very good worker and a very good cook.' Sad to be voted off, Simon remains positive about his two weeks in the inferno. 'Now I'm probably not the terriblest cook,' he says.

7 THE CRITICS HAVE THEIR SAY

'It's very difficult for them ... they are between two teams of killers.' Jean-Christophe Novelli

It's a big night for the remaining trainees. For the first time, their cooking will be picked over, tasted – possibly even spat out – by a party of food critics. Both kitchens know their reputations are on the line. As if that's not enough, the chefs have another treat in store for the trainees at morning roll call.

When the blue team swaggers down – late – they find a po-faced Gary Rhodes waiting for them. 'Not a good start with me,' he says. The chefs have swapped teams for the day.

He wants to know why Kellie thinks she is still in the competition. 'I've listened to everything the chef has said and I've done everything the chef has said,' she says.

'Did you understand everything he said?'

'Only in the last two days, with his accent,' she admits.

Gary decides to set them a challenge. Working to a recipe – a new concept for the blues – they will cook a white pudding.

Terry and Sam arrive for roll call to find Jean-Christophe waiting. 'Oh, oh,' is Sam's reaction.

The chef wonders if they'd have liked to have worked with him over the past couple of weeks. Terry is blunt. 'To be honest, I was pleased I was with Gary Rhodes,' he says.

Jean-Christophe cannot understand how Terry, from Newcastle, could have tolerated working for a chef who supports Manchester United. 'It must have been terrible for you,' he says.

He ushers them into the kitchen – 'the lovely-jubbly blue kitchen' – where their challenge is to make banana caramelised tatin. 'I will let you improvise,' he says. 'Show me some imagination.'

The red trainees start cooking in their new surroundings. 'What a tip,' Terry mutters.

The head chefs are impressed with the standard of the opposition. When Gary Rhodes spots Jean-Christophe showing Sam how to tint a parsnip flower with a piece of beetroot, though, he cannot believe his eyes.

By the evening, though, the teams are back in their rightful place. All the would-be chefs will have a signature dish on that evening's menu. In the blue kitchen, Gary already believes his lamb dish is as good as it can be, but Jean-Christophe wants him to come up with ways of making it even better. Gary is confused. Surely, it is impossible to improve on perfection?

'It was a top seller yesterday. The verdict was a good verdict,' he says, 'so just leave it as it is.'

As he continues with his preparation, though, Jean-Christophe stays close,

keen to bring his culinary expertise to bear on his protégé's creation. 'Why don't you put the mousse on the top?' he suggests. 'And *then* put your basil and your cheese . . .' Gary carries on under the watchful – and unwelcome – eye of his chef. 'It's not enough mousse,' says Jean-Christophe, trying to be helpful. Gary hesitates. 'Unless you *want* it that way,' the chef adds, 'because it's your dish, actually. Do you prefer it that way or do you want to add more mousse?'

Gary, who knew exactly how to prepare his dish the day before, is suddenly having second thoughts. 'The chef's changing my dish,' he says. 'He's all, *Do this* and *Do that*, and I'm just getting all confused and stuck, while he's got his head up his arse.'

Jean-Christophe leaves Gary to it. He's concerned, though, that it's all taking too long. 'It's amazing how slow he is,' says the chef. 'He's a good cook, but he's slow.'

Before the critics arrive, the trainees have a chance to sit down for a few brief moments with their chefs.

Sam tells Gary Rhodes she has had to learn to switch off certain parts of her life – her children, mainly – in order to cope with Hell's Kitchen. 'I haven't been homesick because I've been doing something that I really love,' she tells her mentor. 'I want to do this. I want to make a career for myself.'

It has been tricky for Kellie too, who has also left behind her family. 'I have switched off completely,' she says. 'For once in my life, I've been selfish. I haven't thought about being a mum, I haven't thought about being a wife.'

'It's not selfish,' says Jean-Christophe.

With the winning post in sight, Gary Rhodes wants to know if Terry ever imagined he would get so far.

'Not really, chef,' he says. 'I lack a little bit in self-confidence and I think you've brought a lot of that out now.' In the beginning, Terry was the outsider in the kitchen. 'I think the language thing had a lot to do with it,' he says. 'Coming from the North, there were a lot of southerners here and I really did feel like

an outsider. In the last five days, I've become part of the whole ship.'

Jean-Christophe has detected a huge change in Gary. 'You have the eyes of a killer,' he tells him, impressed.

Gary, who battled with tiredness in the early days of Hell's Kitchen, now feels he has his strength back. 'My mind had to sort my body out and you might be able to see that through my eyes,' he says. 'I've transformed.'

After the defeat of the night before, Gary Rhodes is determined to pull back a win. If he does, the blue kitchen will be unable to catch up. He also knows the food must be up to standard, otherwise the critics will have a field day. He urges the team to stay calm. 'I don't want us to get into any kind of panic just because we have food writers in. As far as I'm concerned, every guest is the same,' he says.

The critics will comprise Fay Maschler and Kate Spicer of the *Evening Standard*, Terry Durack of the *Independent on Sunday*, and Toby Young of the *Mail on Sunday*.

'Toby "I'm-a-complete-dick" Young,' remarks Gary Rhodes. 'He knows bugger all about food and he needs a damn good beating and thrashing from me.'

His fighting spirit continues when there's a mix-up with the red-kitchen orders and the wrong food is served to the wrong tables. The chef rounds on Laura. 'What the hell went on?' he says. 'I can't tell you how goddamn furious I am.'

In the blue kitchen, Jean-Christophe tells his team that Marco Pierre White has called to wish them good luck. Kellie and Gary exchange bemused looks. Marco Pierre Who? 'Is he a footballer?' says Gary.

Jean-Christophe is staggered. 'You must be joking. You don't know Marco Pierre White?'

'We don't follow famous people,' says Kellie.

Jean-Christophe shakes his head in disbelief. 'He was the first English chef to win three Michelin stars,' he says.

They're a bit anxious in the blue kitchen over the critics. Jean-Christophe acknowledges that it cannot be easy for them. 'They are exposed between two very competent teams,' he says. 'Two teams of killers who are going to do everything to win.' The critics decide to order all the specials to share. Not all of the trainees' efforts meet with approval.

'Have you got a bucket?' says Toby Young. 'No question the red side was a lot better than the blue side.' Sam's Succulent Stew scores well for flavour and presentation. Terry's Geordie Treat – Northumberland lamb with redcurrant and mint – also wins praise, although Terry Durack finds it lacking 'thrill value'.

When it comes to the blue team's efforts, the critics sharpen their knives. The special that Gary has toiled over all day is, according to Fay Maschler, spoiled by the presence of Roquefort cheese. Their most savage comments, however, are reserved for Kellie's Rainbow of Hell. 'Actually, it was in a class of its own,' says Terry Durack.

'An anti-class,' adds Kate Spicer. 'Somewhere underneath the cheese, the tomato, the mushrooms, was a nice piece of turbot, but I couldn't taste it because it was so salty and so oily and just wrong.'

It was, according to Fay Maschler, 'a terrible dish, well named. The further one got into it, the more depressed one became.'

Toby Young says, 'I think I'll be seeing it later this evening and I want to examine it in the bottom of the toilet bowl before I give my final verdict.'

When the diners' verdicts come in, both kitchens are tense. The red team has scored eight out of ten. Gary Rhodes breaks into a huge grin. 'We've done it. We can't be caught,' he tells his jubilant team. Jean-Christophe's

team is a point behind. And there is more good news for the red team. The critics have given Sam's special first place. Terry is in second place with his Geordie Treat. Kellie cannot conceal her disappointment. Her dish has come in last.

Jean-Christophe congratulates the rival team, then leads his trainees outside. 'Tonight, *I* lost, you didn't,' he says. 'I didn't keep the team together. Maybe I was a little bit too *egoiste*.'

Both kitchens are about to find out who will compete in the final. The red kitchen is first to hear the result of the public vote. Terry has made it. Sam is on her way home – or at least to a nearby hotel, where Aaron is waiting with champagne and chocolates. She has nothing but praise for her mentor. 'Gary is great. He's a lovely man and he's taught me so much,' she says. 'I'm honoured just to have had the knowledge and experience of working with such a top chef.'

Terry is on an utter high at having reached the final. 'I'm going to try my best to pull it off for Gary, I really am,' he says.

Gary Rhodes is equally delighted to see Terry in the final. 'He is such a wonderful, warm, family man who has a love for cooking,' he says. 'He is definitely a winner.'

The finalist from the blue kitchen is Kellie. Jean-Christophe, overjoyed, lifts her off her feet, as her team-mate Gary prepares to leave. 'She is a born winner,' says Jean-Christophe. 'She's honest – very strong and very genuine. She's natural and she's special.'

In 24 hours, the two finalists will go head-to-head to win *Hell's Kitchen* – and a prize of two hundred and fifty thousand pounds.

'It's a fairy tale ... what dreams are made of.'
Terry Miller, red kitchen trainee

It's the final roll call and Terry and Kellie face their chefs together. In a few hours' time, they will be in charge of their respective kitchens, serving dishes from their own menus. It is a daunting proposition, but both are confident.

'In this short space of time we've taught you more or less everything we could, but now it's down to you,' Gary Rhodes says.

When service begins, he and Jean-Christophe will be in the restaurant having dinner. The finalists will not be without help, however. Their old team-mates troop into the kitchen. Terry and Kellie have to choose three people they want to work with them. Terry picks Aaron and Sam. Kellie goes for Aby and Gary.

Terry struggles to decide between Caroline and Simon. 'Which one is going to help make you a winner?' says Gary Rhodes. He opts for Caroline. Kellie picks her old team-mate Henry. Simon will have the night off. While the others sweat it out over the hotplates, he will be among the Hell's Kitchen diners along with Stein, who is also coming back for dinner.

Both finalists know that they are competing for a rare opportunity. Whatever happens, they will both come away changed people. 'What I've learned off Gary has been invaluable,' says Terry.

'I really think I've come out of this a better person. To win would be like winning the lottery, the FA Cup, *and* having your first child. It's all them things in one.'

For Kellie, Hell's Kitchen has been a roller coaster. 'It's been worth every burn, every cut, and the lack of sleep, to see the improvement from Day One,' she says. 'To win would mean the world to me.'

Each finalist sits down with their chef for a final pep talk. Jean-Christophe tells Kellie she is a winner.

Gary Rhodes wonders if Terry has thought what he might call his restaurant if he wins *Hell's Kitchen*. 'I would probably let me wife pick the name,' he says.

'Wouldn't you call it Rockefeller?' says Gary. 'It would be fantastic, because that's your speciality. That dish, top of the menu, always there. Do you think you're going to win?'

'I think it's very close,' says Terry.

In the blue kitchen, Kellie sets about marshalling her troops. Henry will do starters, Gary will do mains, and Aby will stick with desserts.

'Do you feel like you're going to win?' says Gary. 'You've got faith?'

She nods. 'I know I'll win if you guys are behind me one hundred per cent.' Gary admits he is shattered. She begs

him to give her every bit of energy he can muster for the next few hours.

Jean-Christophe shares Kellie's confidence. 'Running the kitchen is going to be the way she runs her life – no bullshit,' he says. In the red kitchen, Terry briefs his team on starters. 'We've got duck, we've got soup, and . . .' He frowns, his mind a blank. Gary Rhodes gives him a nudge. The other starter is his signature dish, King Prawn Rockefeller. Terry shakes his head. 'I can't believe I forgot me Rockefeller,' he says, laughing.

One of Terry's main concerns is that, in the heat of the moment, his team will struggle to understand him. 'I'm going to try and speak as clear as possible,' he says. 'Can you understand me now?'

They chorus back, 'Yes, chef!'

'I think he's got an awful lot to offer,' says Gary Rhodes. 'He's intelligent, crisp, sharp. He's got a great sense of humour, good cooking abilities, and he leads purely by example. If there's one person I'd really hate to lose, it would be Big Terry.'

If Terry is feeling nervous, he's managing to keep it well hidden. 'He is coping incredibly well,' says Caroline. 'It's rather like being made prefect – you've got to tell the class what to do. I should think he's quite anxious.'

'If you're in control, the nerves shouldn't be there and that's what I need to focus on,' Terry says.

Kellie, too, knows she must not allow nerves to get in the way. 'I can't have any doubt in myself,' she says, 'because it will show in my performance.'

As soon as service begins, though, an order comes in that puts her on the spot. 'They're vegan,' says Laura, 'so no meat, no fish, no butter, no eggs, no cheese.'

Kellie can feel tears prick the back of her eyes. 'My first order – oh my God, it would happen to me.'

'How about some asparagus?' suggests Laura.

In the restaurant, Jean-Christophe tells

Gary Rhodes it has been a pleasure working with him. 'I love you,' says Jean-Christophe. Gary, a bit too British to exchange such intimacies with a man, mutters, 'Cheers. Likewise.'

In the blue kitchen, the team is hampered by a technical problem. One of the freezers is on the blink, and the ice cream is starting to melt. 'Oh my God,' says Aby, 'this is defrosting. We have no desserts. We're buggered.'

Kellie commandeers a red-kitchen freezer. 'Move every dessert over,' she tells her team.

In the red kitchen, service begins well and Terry is proud of the food they're sending out. 'You're doing marvellous,' he tells his team. 'Keep it up.'

Back in the blue kitchen, Kellie reminds Gary to check the turbot with a knife to make sure it's cooked before it goes out. 'Otherwise we could kill someone,' she says.

In the restaurant, Simon tucks into his steak only to find it's not cooked the way he wanted it. It's a bit too pink. At the red-kitchen pass, Laura hands it back to Terry. 'It's Simon's and he's a big supporter of yours. He doesn't want a fuss, but he can't eat it like that. He asked for it medium,' she says.

The turbot Kellie had told Gary to check also lands back at the blue-kitchen pass. 'It went out raw,' she tells him.

Jean-Christophe, watching his kitchen operating in his absence, is impressed. He goes to offer Kellie encouragement. 'I have just realised I'm going to lose my job,' he says. 'I am on the dole. The food was fantastic.'

As the chef prowls around the kitchen, Kellie begs him to leave. 'Don't get us disqualified,' she says.

It's Henry's chance to get his own back on the plate-smashing, spoon-hurling chef. 'Can I just say one thing, chef? F**k off out of the kitchen!'

He does, too.

Morale is breaking down in the red kitchen, where Terry is on the verge of calling in Gary Rhodes. 'You're going to have to help,' he tells Aaron. 'I want you to check the sweets, help

Caroline. There's no main courses on, is there?'

'Just communicate with us and I'll do it,' says Aaron.

Sam, clearly feeling unappreciated, goes outside where she bumps into Kellie. 'We're all working our arses off,' she says, adding, 'I wish *you* all the luck.'

Back in the kitchen, Terry suspects Sam is not pulling her weight. 'Can we get the mullet on, please?' he says.

'Oh, you haven't called it away, chef,' she says.

'I've called it away *twice*,' he tells her. 'Sam, please, or I'll do it myself.'

'A little bit of appreciation wouldn't go amiss,' she mutters.

At the end of service, Terry does his best to smooth things over. 'I know you're not well,' he says, hugging her, 'but I know you tried your best. I love you.'

The head chefs deliver the diners' verdicts to their respective kitchens. The blue team has handled fewer covers – 38 to the red team's 44. There has been a complaint that the blue menu's sorbet was bland and that the salmon was too salty. 'Forget it. It's a dish you excelled in,' says Jean-Christophe. He hugs Kellie. 'You run your kitchen better than me.'

Gary Rhodes tells the red team that someone has complained that there was too much cocoa in the chocolate pudding. 'Odd,' he says, 'because there's no cocoa in it.' Terry's original signature dish – the Rockefeller – wins most compliments. 'Sensational food with Rockefeller dish best of all. Cooking simple with pure class,' Gary Rhodes says. 'Do you know who said that? *Me*.'

As the final votes are cast for the winner of *Hell's Kitchen*, Angus Deayton grabs a quick word with the finalists.

Terry tells him it would be a dream come true to have his own restaurant. 'I thought I was going to be voted off first and here I am in the final,' he says. 'It's just a dream.'

In the space of two weeks, Kellie has mustered every ounce of energy and commitment in the hope of scooping the grand prize. 'I gave my heart, my soul, my passion for food,' she says, 'and I've worked extremely hard.'

With the final votes cast, the two finalists wait for the result. Both look sick with anxiety. 'One of you is about to experience a life-changing event,' says Angus Deayton. 'I can reveal that the person the viewers have decided should be the winner of *Hell's Kitchen* is . . . Terry.'

Gary Rhodes raises his arms in victory. Terry, overwhelmed, covers his face with his hands. The fairy-tale ending he has longed for has come true. A few yards away, his wife Linda is on her feet, clapping and cheering.

As Terry makes his way through the restaurant, applause ringing out around him, he appears dazed. The humble Geordie, who had presented his chef with instant mashed potato on his first day in Hell's Kitchen, has come further than he could ever have imagined. He has only praise for his mentor, Gary Rhodes. 'The respect I've got for him is unbelievable,' he says. 'The guy is just phenomenal. He taught me more in two weeks than I've learned in a lifetime. He's the greatest, and he's my hero.'

He pays tribute to runner-up, Kellie. 'She was fantastic,' he says. 'She's an angel, an absolute star and a hard worker, and I love her to bits.'

As he returns to the red kitchen, he throws his arms around his wife and buries his face in her neck. 'I've done it! I've done it! I've done it!' he tells her.

Wye aye, man.

INDEX